D1744025

Milford Trails

Milford Trails

William Anderson

A. H. & A. W. REED
WELLINGTON • AUCKLAND • SYDNEY • MELBOURNE

First published 1971

A. H. & A. W. REED LTD
182 Wakefield Street, Wellington
29 Dacre Street, Auckland
51 Whiting Street, Artarmon, Sydney
357 Little Collins Street, Melbourne

© 1971 WILLIAM ANDERSON

ISBN 0 589 00472 7

PRINTED BY HALSTEAD PRESS, SYDNEY, AUSTRALIA

CONTENTS

LIST OF ILLUSTRATIONS

7

List of Illustrations

Unless acknowledged, photos are by the author.

LIST OF MAPS

ACKNOWLEDGMENTS

I HAVE EXPERIENCED the most helpful and courteous assistance from the staffs of the Turnbull and Hocken Libraries, the Public Libraries of Auckland, Wellington, Christchurch, Dunedin, Invercargill and from Lands and Survey, Invercargill. Among the many individuals to whom I am indebted are Norman and Lyn Berndtson, Sandy and Mary Brown, Aubrey and Lyndsay Mark, Claude and Rena Hamilton, Arthur and Joan Johnston, Ray and Helen Willett, Mr and Mrs Wally Warhurst, Alan and Hazel Harris, Ida and the late John Rawson, Bill and Joy Hewitt; Mesdames Barbara Roche, J. A. Copp, Betty McRobie, Gladys Mountfort, Hazel McDonald, Misses Peggy Spicer, Judy White-Parsons, Ann Hart, Marlene Rooskov, J. J. Niven; Messrs Ivan Latham, George Pollard, George Auld, Lawson Burrows, Edgar Williams, Peter Howard, D. C. Robertson, Les Smith, Fred Pratt, Phil Turnbull, W. H. Moreton, Graham Hayter, Gerald Beattie, G. R. Cameron, Barney Lang, T. J. Young, Keith Severinsen, Ray O'Brien, Dan Greany, Ken James, Tony Ellis, W. Connelly, Ray Kelly, Marcel von Almen, Tom Milburn, the late Robert Robb, W. Gill, A. McDonald, and A. A. F. Winder, Alan Blake and George Griffiths.

In presenting this book to the reading public, I am mindful of the many good people who contributed to my store of knowledge and in addition to those mentioned here there are doubtless others to whom I am equally indebted. To all I extend my heartfelt thanks and crave pardon from those whose names I have overlooked. I owe much, in the first place, to the many trampers who, displaying so lively an interest in my early scrap books, encouraged me to continue adding to them. Then I must place on record the generous support from the successive managers of Hotels Te Anau and Milford and also the T.H.C. Headquarters staff.

Credit for the initial decision to write the book is largely due to Murray Gunn of Hollyford Camp who, besides giving me much valuable historical material, introduced me to the publishers to whose editor Judith Powell I am indebted for her sound advice and helpfulness.

For illustrations I have leaned heavily on Zygmunt Kepka, who spent much valuable time and spared no pains to secure many of the photographs for the book.

On the home front I have been given encouraging support by my wife Dorothy, who so patiently typed for me and drew the maps.

WILLIAM ANDERSON

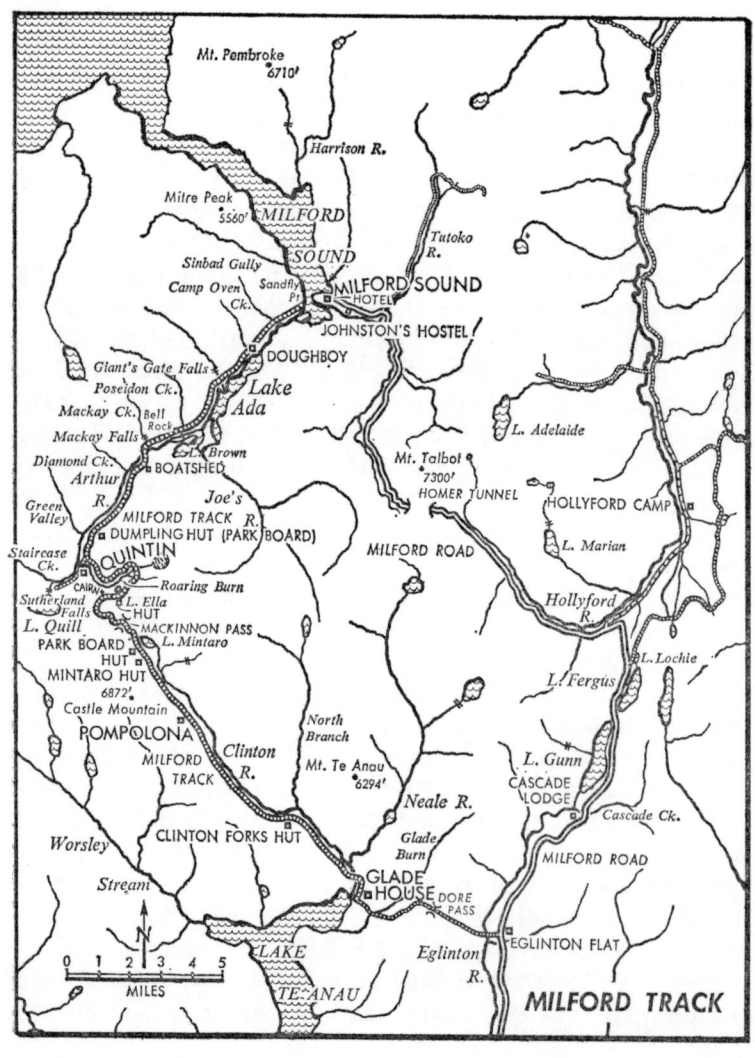

1

A WATERFALL

IN MY GEOGRAPHY BOOK at school there was a picture of the Sutherland Falls, not an impressive one; but, because this waterfall was described as the highest in the world, I resolved I must see it some day.

The Milford Track, I thought, was only the way to "The Falls" and Milford Sound. It didn't seem likely it could boast of any very special features of its own. My little world at that time was enough and satisfying; there was no hurry to look farther away for something bigger and brighter. To one who had been no further than seven miles from home, the Sutherland Falls seemed as far off as another country and could very well wait.

Our farm, where I was born, was in Western Southland, on the eastern side of the Pourakino River, not far from Riverton. The homestead sheltered in the lee of "Birch Bush".

Like any normal young person, at an early age I felt the urge to explore and find new places and before I reached school age I made the most of my opportunities to explore and find adventure. My mother was convinced I took too great advantage of my liberty and threatened to tie me to the leg of the kitchen table if I didn't do something about curbing my walkabout instincts.

One of these excursions, which I can just faintly remember, led me to a place where manuka and great, flowing red tussocks reached far above my head. Here, as I looked around, the unaccustomed quietness and stillness began to frighten me and I turned and ran for home as fast as my legs could carry me.

Another time I was spotted making a getaway when my sister ran up to head me off. Coming to the edge of the bush with a red coat over her head and making blood-curdling noises like those of an enraged bull, she turned me on my tracks with a sprint for home that still holds the record for a rising four-year-old.

My mother's threat to tie me up had not proved a sufficient deterrent so I was made to suffer the ignominy of being tied to the table leg. I got off lighter than I deserved, for only this once and not for long was I subjected to that humiliating treatment.

When I reached school age, exploratory excursions with my older brother became more orderly. The Milford Track was far away but we had the bush and tracks of our own to follow, where deep in the twilight shade an overpowering sense of mystery lingered and where imagination and perception quickened to an awareness of kinship between the spirit of life in the tree and our own. We had no kiwis or wekas, but our bush was alive with birds. An unbroken chorus of song greeted us in the early morning, while a more subdued performance in the evening tapered off to the last sleepy, contented cheep. Parrakeets by the score found nesting places in holes in the trunks of ancient beeches, and in the fruiting season came down in flocks to the gooseberry bushes. Columns of starlings, miles long, made their way home in late afternoon, in some of their massed flight movements making music in the sky with their whirring wings. In the dusk, owls, and the more numerous bats made their silent flight.

Our river was tidal and as unlike a madly rushing Fiordland torrent as could be, but we were able to explore the pools left by the receding tide on the mudflats and look for treasures abandoned at the high-water mark.

Nearby was the great Longwood forest where we sometimes accompanied our father on game shooting excursions. Through a gap in the Longwood Hills we could see the Takitimu Mountains, and somewhere beyond them the great Sutherland Falls leaped, played and crashed into a deep Fiordland valley.

Within this limited horizon I found complete satisfaction, but the time came when I began to learn more of the wider world and in particular, the glories of the Milford Track. I came to know several people who had walked the track and gradually understood that the reason for its fame came not entirely from that great showpiece, the Sutherland Falls.

My interest increased when a neighbour, Stewart Robertson, lent us McHutcheson's *Camp Life in Fiordland*. Stewart told us that the character known in the book as Rob Roy was his father, George Robertson who, after swagging round the country on foot, shearing, harvesting, or accepting any job offering, finally settled down in a prosperous business in Riverton. His exploits as Rob Roy on the Milford Track, as a JP and elder of the kirk in his home town make a varied combination of accomplishments.

Reading of his exploits in the Milford area started off an urge to follow in his footsteps and, one day, to see for myself this wonderful country.

As a young man at a house party in the home of John Ross, at one time a Milford Track guide, I was told by the local fortune-teller that I was to make a sea voyage very soon. That sort of talk of course we expect from a fortune-teller, but in a few weeks I was away with the First Expeditionary Force to the Great War.

After being wounded at the ridge called The Rhododendron at Gallipoli I was sent from hospital in Alexandria to England. On recovery I went back to Egypt and then to France where I was soon part of the battle of the Somme. In France I was posted to the infantry stretcher bearers and in this capacity served until wounded again. I returned home early in 1918, and in the absence of my brothers in camp and at the war, I was kept busy on the farm. A younger brother, Robert, did not return. He fell at the Somme.

Late in 1919 I married and settled on a farm near the home farm. After some years we sold this farm and bought one near Invercargill. When our sons took over this farm after World War II, we felt free to cast our eyes farther afield for interest, occupation and pleasure. Our family of three boys and two girls were never surprised at anything their parents did and our proposed new life met with no opposition from them.

Among inviting alternatives, the Milford Track still beckoned and would have called us at some time, even if we had not seen an advertisement in the paper for a couple to manage Quintin Huts for a short time near the close of the 1949-50 season. We were not serious about the idea when we went to Invercargill that morning, but, in passing the Tourist Office, we decided to pop in and see what the job was about. An interview with the manager, Mr Bailey, convinced us that by taking the job we would see more of the track by working on it than by walking it. Our "No" when he asked if we had done any of that sort of work before, did not worry him when he learned of our farming background. We both belonged to large families, May, the third in a family of eleven, myself sixth in a family of nine, which at harvest time were often augmented to the size of a track party. In the mid-summer school vacation droves of holidaying youngsters would put in an appearance and bring with them a healthy appetite. We had known the days of large social gatherings and house parties, which needed catering that would make the modern housewife gasp.

We asked Mr Bailey when he wanted us to go in if we accepted the position. His reply was, "Tomorrow". The Quintin couple had walked out, giving scant notice and, although the track staff under the foreman J. A. B. (Sandy) Brown were coping successfully, the sooner the situation was remedied the better.

Tomorrow, we thought, was a bit sudden, so we bargained for two or three days later. He told us we would not be satisfied with one visit to the Sutherland Falls, and I am sure no truer words have been spoken, for after scores of visits over the intervening years, for me it has lost none of its original attraction. One other significant observation he made was that we would find the type and character of the people walking the track, more pleasant than in some other resorts. With this, also, we were to agree.

Back at home, hurried preparation for leaving gave little time for reflection, and it was only when we boarded the bus for Milford that we really felt committed to this escapade.

2

ANTICIPATION AND REALISATION

THE TOWNSHIP OF LUMSDEN, fifty miles from Invercargill, is more important than its size. Here the north-south road and rail (Invercargill-Queenstown) are crossed by the east-west highway linking Gore with Te Anau. The railway on the same route ends at Mossburn some twelve miles farther. At Lumsden, we found the usual bustle among travellers converging from the four corners to disperse again in as many directions as they had come.

So primitive were travelling conditions at an earlier time that adventure started where the rail journey ended here at Lumsden or Mossburn. No account of a visit to Fiordland excluded many incidents on the approach to the lakes. But in March 1950 we travelled more comfortably.

When we left the Invercargill-Queenstown Highway at the road and rail bridge over the Oreti, we entered unfamiliar country. Some people find this route monotonous but the novelty of this, our first time over it, appealed to us. The gravelled road was rough in places and dust in generous measure invaded the bus and settled on the young, the old, the lordly and the humble with impartial favour. We took this treatment as a matter of course and considered how well off we were compared with earlier travellers.

Present-day travellers on a first-class road and in modern cars may pity those of an earlier age, but such pity is quite misplaced. The spice of danger in fording swollen streams and following tracks and roads likely to bog or overturn a vehicle, accompanied by the coachman's running commentary, made first-class copy for memories to treasure for life. The foot-slogger in rain and mud, or sweltering in the summer's heat, the traveller in the open chaise, had the compensating delights of the friendly welcome, the homely fireside and generous board of the old-time hotels of Lumsden, Mossburn, Centre Hill, the Key and Te Anau. Here as elsewhere the motor spelt their doom. The country asked for something more up-to-date, and therefore got it, but something is lacking.

15

Crossing the Mararoa River we left the wilderness of tussock country to enter one of another kind. "The Wilderness", the name given most appropriately to this desert area, is unique: it supports little growth other than *Dacrydium bidwillii* or bog pine we were told. Here, the bus driver told us, a specimen of the rare takahe was found in 1897 and sold to the Berlin Museum.

The Te Anau we saw in 1950 was very different from the one we know today. It was swallowed up in the all-pervading manuka and fern, but the open waterfront with its blue gums, kowhais, and poplars rescued it from suffocation and gave it a distinctive character that possibly was not designed or anticipated by the worthy citizens who planted them.

After a short stop we were on the way again heading for Milford. Looking back from this angle I could understand the reason for the name Takitimu being conferred on the bold mountain range in the distance. The *Takitimu*, one of the canoes in the fleet which brought the Maoris from their distant home to New Zealand, was wrecked at Te Waewae Bay. From their village at Blue Gum Point, these imaginative people saw in each peak a warrior with his paddle, in the outline of the mountain the canoe, while the plains were its sails.

After the wilderness of fern and manuka it was a welcome change to enter Ten Mile Bush as the road ran up the lakeside. We hear much about the hand of man despoiling nature, but in the Te Anau area he uses one of nature's drab canvases to paint the most beautiful pictures of green terraces and slopes, contented sheep and cattle in fields framed with neat regular fences and adorned by attractive homes, soon to be surrounded by sheltering trees. From the rise at Te Anau Downs where Parker's well-appointed roadhouse now stands is a very pleasing view of the bay and we have found that when the willows are turning colour, few with a camera can pass without taking more than the memory of it with them.

Continuing on through scrub and fern we reached the grassy flats and clumps of bush, forerunner of the heavy dense beech forest. If my artistic sensibilities were not sufficiently alive to appreciate beauty in bracken and magnificence in manuka as here displayed in its blighted disarray, they responded to the forest we then entered. At that time a greater distance into the forest could be seen from the road, as side growth had not filled in to any extent and overhead, where then there was the wide open sky, the trees are now meeting. Narrow road, narrow bridges, sharp turns with blind corners and all the crudities associated with a road of this nature have been and still are being eliminated.

From the Divide at 1,740 feet, the magnificent view looking down and over the Lower Hollyford Valley took us by surprise with its great sweep of beech forest spread at our feet, and with its turbulent river and rearing peaks.

Entering the narrow valley of the Upper Hollyford the huge bare mountainsides close in, making one aware of one's littleness. At Falls Creek the bus paused to give us a better view of that most striking cataract. As we drove up the steep incline to the Homer tunnel, rain we had met earlier turned to a brisk snow shower. At that time the bus stopped at the foot of the hill leading to the tunnel entrance. There the passengers got out and walked through it. They were met by another bus on the Milford side some distance down the road from the tunnel. The hotel truck met the bus on the Hollyford side and, as we were privileged staff, we rode in it through the tunnel and down to the hotel.

Lowering clouds over the waters of the Sound and the shambles of the burnt-out wing of the hotel did nothing to impress us with the far-famed beauty of Milford, but at the same time it did not weaken our interest in the surroundings.

On arrival at Milford we were welcomed by Mr and Mrs Berndtson, the manager and his wife, who told us about our new job. Their advice, their generous support and understanding we felt we could always rely upon, nor was this first impression ever proved wrong. In the morning we set off by launch to Sandfly Point to see for the first time the famous Milford Track.

The head of the Sound is magnificent in scenic beauty and on this clear morning we feasted on it. But in addition, the view up the Arthur Valley, with the sharp peak of Mt McKenzie in the distance at its head, seemed to beckon and to contain all the mystery of a new world and the promise of fulfilment of my early expectations. With the passing years mystery had given place to reality, anticipation to realisation but with every glance up that valley from Milford an answering call like an echo strikes a chord as strongly today as it did on that first clear look I had of it.

At Sandfly the establishment had two buildings, a hut containing the telephone, two bunks, stove, a table and chair, while a larger

17

building used as a stable, chaff and storeroom had also another room attached which was filled with odds and ends. These buildings told a tale of earlier days when Sandfly catered for the track parties. This was before the hotel was opened in Milford in 1928.

A trolley line ran from the jetty to the stable and cargo from the launch was either delivered along it to the storeroom or loaded straight on to the backs of the packhorses. A fence and gateway just clear of the jetty was a necessary inconvenience, for the horses were always on the lookout for a chance to make their escape to Milford. Another fence two or three hundred yards up the track limited their wanderings in that direction.

I gave a hand with the stores before setting off with my wife up the track, leaving Jack Sullivan, the Lake Ada boatman and Jock Peterson, the packer, to follow with the packhorses.

At Doughboy we all embarked on the old Lake Ada boat, a somewhat barge-shaped, but good, sound, safe, cargo carrier built of kauri. As we made our way up the lake we were busily looking in all directions at the scenery and listening to Jack Sullivan's tales. I was especially impressed by Giant's Gate, that deep cleft between the mountains through which the flowing waters make the superb waterfall of that name. I felt for the first time, though certainly not the last, the cold waters of the Arthur River when, at the rapids, I had to jump in and push and pull when there wasn't depth enough for the outboard motor to operate.

At Boatshed, where we disembarked, we found a track party relaxing in various postures in and around the building, waiting for the boat to ferry them across the river after it had discharged its load. They were ferried across three-quarters of a mile farther down the river.

At times I think everyone keeps some small picture while more important ones fade away. What I remember most about this is a pair of boots. Trivial is perhaps not the most appropriate word that could be used about a pair of boots, standing on their heels, appearing like a road-block and almost hiding the wearer sitting behind them, a girl, of only medium stature. How she managed to propel those heavy weights over the miles of track from Te Anau was a mystery to me. Here we met John Pollard, the packer from Quintin, who had prepared and served the numerous cups of tea to the tramping party and who gave us some.

We set off on the last five-and-a-half-mile lap to Quintin, going ahead of John and his horses. All the way up the track we were reminded of the big pair of boots which had left cleat-marks like those of a traction engine. Where the track led off to the horse ford at Roaring Creek, we were momentarily puzzled which way to take. Those footprints coming towards us soon put us right.

The first time over a track usually seems the longest and we shared the feeling of most trampers that the miles up here were longer than those we had been used to elsewhere. But, although they seemed stretched, we were too interested to feel tired and on this bright, sunshiny day our impressions equalled our expectations.

When we arrived at Quintin we were in for some surprises. Emerging from the bush we saw the building in the clearing all right, but not exactly as we expected to find it. What was obviously the main entrance, for it bore a "Welcome" sign above the door, was fenced off by a line running obliquely across the track and draped with empty coal and chaff sacks, optimistically hung there to dry. Instead of ducking under these rather filthy objects we made our way round the end of the building to see if there was another entrance. Round the corner of the building we came face to face with a horse approaching at full gallop with a log flailing about in its wake. The sudden appearance of two strangers diverted it from its accustomed course and spurred it on to put up an impromptu performance that left us gasping.

It took off among the bushes like a whirlwind, hurling fragments of branches, leaves, sticks and fern into the air. Presently George Pollard came up the track with an axe on his shoulder, and the horse stopped as if struck with a tranquilliser and allowed him to detach the log. None of the horses were broken to the collar and the drill was for one man to hold the horse while another attached the load. On this occasion, knowing that it was going to be pursued by a great tail-lashing reptile, the horse had plunged and reared and one descending hoof had ripped off George's leather belt. Immediately the drag-chain was fixed, the horse was released, and the attendant sprang into the bush for safety. The two or three hundred yards the horse had to cover were not sufficient to tire it or reduce its speed. But when it reached the firewood heap it stopped dead and calmly waited for the woodcutter to come and release it. By these spectacular means the fires of Quintin were fed.

We turned and found a door opening into the kitchen. Dinner was well on the way and we were not allowed to do anything to help. We would have it all to ourselves in the morning. Sandy Brown was in charge and had as a casual assistant one of the hotel staff. She had come up to Quintin to spend her days off and was making herself useful.

Next morning, with some misgivings, we started our first day, but found the temporary crew had left everything in good running order, while the track staff and guests were as helpful and co-operative as we could wish. With the breakfast rush over we were able to look around the place. The tall forest trees that had originally stood on the site of Quintin had been cut back to make a clearing of about two acres, but second growth had taken their place and grew to within a few yards of the building.

To the west the ground sloped down to the Arthur River some 200 yards away, while to the east Roaring Creek was quite near. The sound of its waters was ever present in our ears. The majestic Mt McKenzie, towering above the nearby peaks, stood at the head of the Arthur Valley. Pillans, to its right, sombrely overlooked our habitation. In the distance, at the head of Green Valley, the enchantingly beautiful Lady of the Snows gave distinction and character to the view that needed little to complete it. The Edgar Mountains, the spur of Mt Elliot, the tip of Mt Balloon, the MacKinnon Pass and Mt Hart filled in the remainder of the horizon which our heads had to be tilted to an unusual angle to follow.

Next to the main building of kitchen, store, manager's quarters, dining-room, men's and women's dormitories, ablution section, drying-rooms and engine-room, were the track staff hut and laundry, while the stable, with no apologies for its weathered appearance, presided over the scattered growth in the clearing and the rough barbed wire corral which all but surrounded it.

Sandy introduced me to the engine-room and enlightened me on the troubles I could encounter and how to overcome them. A remarkably staunch three-and-a-half-horsepower single cylinder engine and a two-kilowatt generator provided DC current for light and power. There was a very good heating system for the drying-rooms and for the water for the showers, but its use was limited by the quantity of petrol and diesel we had. There was always the need to conserve fuel. The five transport stages by land and water between Hotel Milford and Quintin meant a lot of handling and a lot of hard work for man and beast bringing in the stores, so all that was delivered was very precious.

Quintin at that time accommodated forty guests, twenty in each of two dormitories containing double-tier bunks. Ladies, however, were usually in the majority and at times additional stretchers were needed in their dormitory.

With the minimum of elbow room, two dozen could be seated at the dining-table. Two sittings were usually needed, but generally diners for whom there was no room at the table, preferred not to wait but to pick up their meal and eat it elsewhere. The kitchen was very small and often crowded with unbidden but willing volunteers to help with the cleaning up. While the book of rules was silent on this subject, we found that by occasionally allowing them to help, we were giving them as much pleasure as they were giving us, for it gave them the feeling of belonging to the place and helped to break down the aloofness between staff and guests that should have no place in out-of-the-way places like Quintin.

The track staff dined in the kitchen and after their breakfast at 7.30 we had to have the table cleared to serve the 8 o'clock invasion by the guests. The range had only one oven functioning and never enough room on top for the necessary pots and pans, but May resourcefully always had meals served on time and satisfied all comers.

The storeroom was well stocked. Supplies arrived up to time and were plentiful. Trampers, particularly the young, work up a great appetite and are genuinely appreciative of the generous helpings served them.

As soon as we could we went up to see the Sutherland Falls. I had expected, from descriptions I had heard, a very impressive sight, but what I saw left me breathless. Admittedly I saw them to advantage with a more than normal flow. The rasping, volleying sounds and dense driving spray added a quality I had not expected, and with the grandeur of the surroundings it was an extraordinary experience. It is unfortunate that many trampers, tired at the end of a hard day, make a hurried trip before dinner and see the falls at the least favourable time, when the sun has left and when they are too tired to appreciate them.

At that time three regular parties a week walked the Track. Leaving Te Anau about 8 am, they reached the head of the lake about noon. They lunched at Glade House then walked to Pompolona, taking a full afternoon to do the ten miles. The next day, over the pass to Quintin and including a visit to the Sutherland Falls entailed a near twelve-mile tramp and this made the hardest of the three-day hike between Lake Te Anau and Milford Sound. The last day's performance, thirteen miles, descending from 830 feet to sea level, was not too hard if they kept an even pace. Having their midday lunch at Boatshed, many had the impression that half the day's walk was over. With two miles more to cover than in the morning, many found they had to speed up to get to Sandfly in time for the launch.

Before the season ended my wife and I went up to the Mac-Kinnon Pass. The day was perfect, and I said to May, "Come on, this is too good to waste. Let's go up to the pass."

"So it is," answered May. "And it's also ideal for the washing. We'll have to get that done first."

Despite my wish to get away early, I could see her point and we turned to. But with the usual heavy load it was lunchtime before the chores were done and the clothes lines filled. With a backward look from May at her morning's work flapping satisfactorily behind us, we set off.

As we neared Crows' Nest Hut, two miles from Quintin, we heard a cooee from across the valley under Mt Balloon. I cooeed back, and soon after we met George Pollard on his way back to Quintin from Pompolona. We were pleased to meet him, and May doubly so as it would be late by the time we got back. Ever mindful of her duties, she asked George if he would mind taking in the washing. George cheerfully promised to do this and as we went on I said to May, "Now you can forget all about your work and enjoy yourself."

The zigzag track seemed as if it would never lead us to the top of the pass. Every now and then we stopped to look back over the valley, picking out the track we had followed over the moraine down past the little dot in the distance which was the Crows' Nest. The higher we climbed the more impressed we were by the great cirque at the head of the valley, while the Jervois Glacier with its icy cliffs and extensive field glittered in the clear atmosphere of the bright afternoon sun.

The afternoon was wearing on when we reached a place from where we could look down on Quintin far below on the floor of the Arthur Valley. Our gaze took in the beautiful Green Valley with the lovely Lady of the Snows at its head and numerous other peaks. I expectantly awaited May's reaction to all this magnificence, when she turned to me with an anxious—"Can you see if the washing has been brought in?" A mere male will never understand the devotion of the laundress to her art.

The season drew quietly to its close. John Pollard took all our luggage beyond what we could carry in a pack, before the horses were taken to Milford for the winter. Our last guest arrived from Milford the day before we went out. He carried a movie camera, the first I had seen on the Track. George Pollard remained to assist in draining the water off and leaving everything tidy. The day was fine and we enjoyed the cruise down the river and lake. The main exodus of the Hotel Milford staff for the winter was taking place, and as a chef was needed for a short time to cook for the skeleton staff, my wife and I remained to fill the gap, she as chef, myself as kitchen hand, to oblige the Berndtsons who had treated us so generously.

We came out from Milford before the first winter snows had fallen, with our minds fully made up to go back to the Track the next season. The one visit that we thought would suffice, only whetted our appetites for more. The variety of scenery, its appearance altering with the ever-changing atmospheric conditions, the variety in alpine and lowland plant life, in river, lake, mountain— and, more entertaining than all, the novelty of contact with people from every corner of the globe and from every walk of life, this was only dimly visualised before we came, if indeed we thought of it at all. In looking forward to the next season there were new vistas that stretched away into the haze and mists of a beckoning horizon, a world of promise, of endless opportunity to repay in useful service the great privilege gained by citizenship of this unique kingdom.

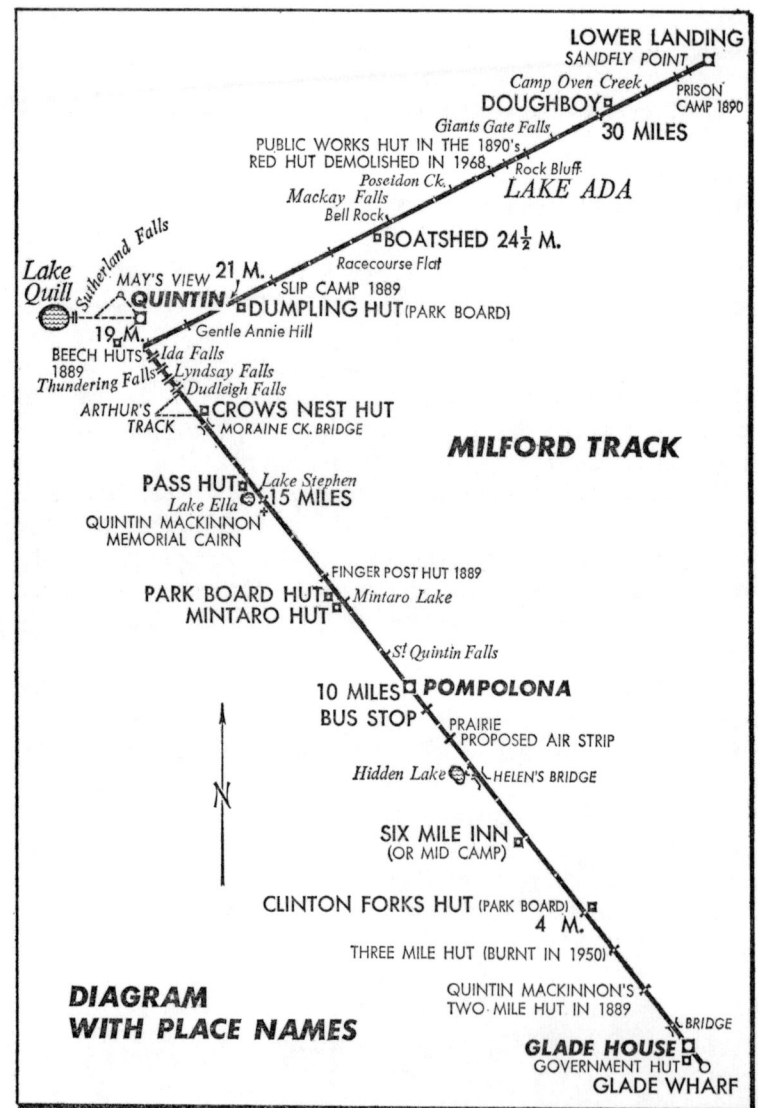

LOWER LANDING
SANDFLY POINT
Camp Oven Creek   PRISON
DOUGHBOY   CAMP 1890
30 MILES
Giants Gate Falls
PUBLIC WORKS HUT IN THE 1890's
RED HUT DEMOLISHED IN 1968.   Rock Bluff
Poseidon Ck.   *LAKE ADA*
Mackay Falls
Bell Rock
BOATSHED 24½ M.
Racecourse Flat
Lake 21 M.
Quill   MAY'S VIEW   SLIP CAMP 1889
QUINTIN   DUMPLING HUT (PARK BOARD)
19 M.   Gentle Annie Hill
BEECH HUTS   Ida Falls
1889   Lyndsay Falls
Thundering Falls   Dudleigh Falls
ARTHUR'S   CROWS NEST HUT
TRACK   MORAINE CK. BRIDGE   **MILFORD TRACK**

PASS HUT   Lake Stephen
Lake Ella   15 MILES
QUINTIN MACKINNON
MEMORIAL CAIRN

FINGER POST HUT 1889
PARK BOARD HUT   Mintaro Lake
MINTARO HUT

St Quintin Falls

10 MILES   **POMPOLONA**
BUS STOP   PRAIRIE
PROPOSED AIR STRIP

Hidden Lake   HELEN'S BRIDGE

N

SIX MILE INN
(OR MID CAMP)

CLINTON FORKS HUT (PARK BOARD)
4 M.
THREE MILE HUT (BURNT IN 1950)

DIAGRAM   QUINTIN MACKINNON'S
WITH PLACE NAMES   TWO·MILE HUT IN 1889
BRIDGE
GLADE HOUSE
GOVERNMENT HUT
GLADE WHARF

3

IN THE BEGINNING

A QUESTION FREQUENTLY asked by Track patrons is "When did the Milford Track first come into use?" When informed that it began with the discovery of the MacKinnon Pass in 1888, that reply, far from satisfying, merely prompts further questions, until step by step, question and answer reach back to the first act in the story.

When I made my first acquaintance with the Milford Track in 1950, my own ignorance of its earlier history was profound. For my own satisfaction, as well as that of Track patrons, I started gathering items of historical interest and put them into scrap books. From this labour I have acquired material for a detailed story of the Track from the earliest beginnings.

The search for a pass giving access to Milford Sound from the interior took in the open ranges above the bushline and up the deep, glacier-formed valleys to their heads, buried out of sight on either side of the Southern Alps. There the ramparts between the valley heads proved insurmountable although some, like the Homer, were comparatively narrow. The search went on until there remained to be investigated only the Clinton Valley in the east and Roaring Creek, a tributary of the Arthur River in the west.

The Maoris, of course, were familiar with the route via these valleys. Not enough credit has been given them for their enterprise in exploration, or credence to the information they were able to furnish the early exploring Europeans. Captain Howell, the founder of Riverton and master of the whaling station there, was told by the southern Maoris that they reached Milford Sound by way of the Waiau Valley and Lake Te Anau. It is true that the Clinton Valley and Roaring Creek were not easily accessible, nevertheless it seems strange that in the light of this knowledge these valleys were the last to be explored.

The story of the exploits of the Maoris in this region is more colourfully embellished than that of their white brothers. They say that their great god Tu-te-Rakiwhanoa hacked out Milford Sound from the solid granite mountains. Unfortunately he was called away before he had completed a pathway between the Cleddau and Hollyford valleys, blocked by the Homer Saddle, and this job was left in the hands of a minor god, Ruru. In his inexperience Ruru hacked at the bottom, instead of from the top of the cliff. Getting nowhere with the job, he went round to the other side, but here he employed the same futile tactics. In disgust he left Te Kohaka-o-te-ruru for an easier saddle to work on and his choice fell on Omanui (the MacKinnon Pass). Here he avoided the mistake he had made at Homer and worked from the top. He was getting along fine with the job till in over-eagerness he missed out some vital passage in the invocation which inspired the work. All his frantic efforts to complete the job were then of no avail. That is the reason we are now obliged to climb over its 3,600 feet.

As far as Europeans are concerned, the story begins with their discovery of Milford Sound, but not by Captain Cook who sailed past without suspecting that beyond the unlikely-looking entrance lay the most magnificent of all the sounds. Once the whalers and sealers came on the scene, however, it could not long remain hidden. Captains John Grono and Peter Williams may not have been first among these to visit it, but it was they who made it known to the world. John Grono is credited with naming the sound Milford Haven after his birthplace in Wales. Other Welsh names bestowed on prominent features were St Anne's Point, Cleddau River, Llawrenny, and Pembroke Mountains.

From this time (1823) onwards, Milford Sound became well-known and earned the highest praise from all sea-going masters. Here was a safe haven from the Tasman storms, a magnificent harbour and entrancing scenery.

In 1848 John Lort Stokes, commanding the paddle steamer *Acheron*, began the survey of the New Zealand coastline and harbours. The *Acheron* reached Milford Sound in 1851. The more than favourable report following this survey was not overlooked by the founders of the new Otago settlement. Here was a potentially ideal port to serve Western Otago. Its nearness to Australia in comparison with the main New Zealand ports, and its scenic attractions which would draw welcome tourists with money to spend, was too great an asset to neglect.

26

In the Beginning

The *Philip Laing*, one of the first two vessels which brought the Otago settlers to New Zealand (among whom was my grandfather) had to take shelter from the storm at Milford Haven in Wales. It may be that their own new Milford Haven would do as much to nurse and establish their young, struggling settlement. With these visions to encourage them, the Otago Provincial Council in May 1863 chartered the seventeen-ton schooner-rigged yacht *Matilda Hayes* to convey an exploratory and geological expedition to Milford Sound. Its chief errand was to discover, if possible, a suitable route for a railway through the mountains bordering the Sound. Doctor (later Sir James) Hector was placed in command. With him in the ship's company were Williams, assistant geologist, Mr Hutchison, owner of the yacht, J. Falconer, captain, J. Walsh, chief mate, Mr Jorden, carpenter, W. Boer, coxswain, Henry Parramata, pilot, W. Walker, A.B., and Joe, an Italian cook.

The expedition spent from 7 to 25 August at Milford and, during that time, explored the Cleddau Valley and followed its tributaries to their heads. In his report Hector does not mention exploring the Arthur Valley, but he knew of the lake two miles up the river from its mouth, which he named Abraham. The shores of this lake, later renamed Ada, by Sutherland, were possibly the last home of some remnants of the lost tribe. Traces of these fugitives were found in 1872 when Kupa Haeroroa and a number of other Maoris from Colac Bay in Southland left their boats at the head of the Sound on one of their sealing expeditions to explore the valley of the Arthur River. They imagined at first that they were the first to come upon this lovely lake but, not far from the mouth of the Arthur River, they were astonished to discover three prints of naked feet in the mud beneath a cliff.

In several places along the shores of Lake Ada they found indications of primitive habitation. Under overhanging rock shelters they came upon deserted sleeping places, surrounded by rows of stones and ashes of cooking fires. At one of these camps, a separate and smaller sleeping place, somewhat apart from the others, suggested the bed of a chief.

While Hector's expedition was unsuccessful in achieving its chief objective, the report of its activities and a description of the scenery resulted in intensified exploration of the wide region lying between Lakes Te Anau and Wakatipu. Runholders, looking for grazing areas, miners for minerals and surveyors engaged in their rugged pioneer tasks, all had visions of discovering an open way to Milford Sound.

Among the first of these to reach Lake Te Anau were Messrs C. J. Nairn, a runholder, and W. Stephens, a son of Dunedin's first judge, who reached the southern end of the lake on 26 January 1852. Some give John McKay the credit for being the first. He very well could have been but we are not in possession of supporting evidence such as Nairn left in his diary.

Earlier, in 1861, Messrs Griffiths and Henry explored the Eglinton Valley, reaching the vicinity of Knobbs Flat. In the same year George Gunn and David McKellar, coming from Lake Wakatipu, reached the Key Summit, and looked down on the lakes in Eglinton Valley. Their exploits find permanent record in the lakes that bear their respective names.

In 1862 James McKerrow surveyed Lake Te Anau and its three arms. He gave the name Clinton to the river so well-known to trampers on the Milford Track. In 1867 Samuel Moreton and W. Y. H. Hall, both of Invercargill, the former an artist, visited Lake Te Anau and rowed their boat the full length of the lake and up the Clinton two miles to where Quintin MacKinnon later erected his hut. There they went ashore, but finding evidence of floodwater feet high on the trees, did not prolong their stay.

While pressure was being kept up from inland there was a pause in exploration from the sea. Activity in the Sound itself however continued. The vessel *Geelong* (Captain Thomas Hart) may be noted for the doubtful honour of liberating rabbits on the Cleddau Delta, in late 1867 or early 1868. Seemingly they did not thrive for we hear no more of them.

HMS *Clio* with the Governor of New Zealand, Sir George Bowen on board, visited the Sounds in 1871. He was honoured by the bestowal of his name on the magnificent waterfall at the head of the Sound. The Stirling Falls, in their turn honour the commander of the *Clio*.

We will now skip a few years and reach a momentous event in the history of the Sound, and of the (as yet) unknown Milford Track. This was the arrival of Donald Sutherland on 9 December 1877. His life had been an adventurous one. Born in 1840 in Wick, Scotland, he had from an early age evinced an urge to wander and see the world.

At twelve years of age he had run away from home on his first escapade, but found the world a harder place than he had expected, so back he went to think over the lesson he had learned and to toughen up for the next encounter. After a brief two years he left home for good, first to sea, then to join Garibaldi's army in Italy. The sea called him again, and after a time he looked for a change, so, finding himself in New Zealand waters with more fighting in sight, he enlisted as a militiaman. At the conclusion of the Maori Wars he served on the government steamer *Stella* which included Milford Sound in its itinerary. So powerfully was he impressed on his first visit with the grandeur of its scenery that he vowed if ever he came to anchor, this would be the place. Subsequent visits seemed only to deepen his first impressions, so it was with a mind made up to forsake his wandering existence that he stepped ashore and commenced to build what he fondly called the City of Milford. With sealskins to barter for supplies from the occasional vessel which called, and his larder augmented by the plentiful fish and game, he found complete satisfaction in this primitive mode of living. Here he felt he was "monarch of all he surveyed" and, it is believed, was not eager to see a way opened up to his domain from the interior which might lead to any lowering of his status.

He had been to the Gabriel Gully goldrush and had spent some time mining at Coromandel and on the West Coast. Here at Milford he continued to pursue the quest for minerals of marketable value.

Sutherland, the first white man actually to live in this region, was the link with pioneer exploration days, for in the next forty years he carried on the investigations of Hector, his most famous achievement being the discovery of the Sutherland Falls. He also cut the first track up the Arthur Valley, and ran the guesthouse and a launch on the lake for many years.

With his dog Johnny Groat, his sole companion, Sutherland lived in a tent while he built his hut of slabs and thatch, adorned with his nameplate, "D. Sutherland, No. 1 Rotorua Street, 4/11/78".

For nine months this well-travelled man lived content with his hermit existence, his days satisfyingly filled with exploring, fishing, hunting and mineral prospecting. The solitude suited this unchallenged ruler over his vast kingdom, about which he had some rather unusual ideas. He was convinced of the fabulous value of its mineral wealth; gold, diamonds, rubies, greenstone and asbestos were there for the gathering.

He sent word, after nine months of solitary splendour, to John Mackay, a prospector at Big Bay, inviting him to join him in asbestos and greenstone prospecting at Anita Bay. In about 1880 the two were joined by James Malcolm, whose father captained the coasting vessel *Mari*. Two more huts rose beside the first, and the three men lived together in the settlement Sutherland proudly called "The City of Milford". Malcolm's brother joined them for a time but neither stayed long. The great mining venture failed, and the settlement was reduced to two. Sutherland still continued prospecting and it was on one of these excursions, accompanied by John Mackay, that he turned his attention to the Arthur Valley.

They would have found the going pretty tough as anyone may judge by the terrain alongside the Track. Beyond Lake Ada they were in virgin territory and their first great reward was a beautiful waterfall, very impressive in its rugged setting. To determine who should have the privilege of naming it they tossed a coin. Mackay won and conferred upon it his name.

Pressing on, they found after a time the grade becoming steeper. The river, comparatively placid for several miles above the lake, now began to foam and make music among the boulders. The tangled growth they had forged their way through on the lower levels thinned out as they entered the heavy beech forest. Their route nevertheless became more difficult with the steepening grade and the rough and rocky nature of the forest floor. Finally, their encounter with the hill we now know as Gentle Annie, might have made them think that whatever they found at the top would need to be pretty good to reward them for their exertions.

Their tired limbs and jaded spirits, ready to call a halt and beat a retreat, were soon to be electrified into fresh energy when, a short distance beyond the top of the hill, the intervening spur of Mt Pillans fell back to reveal a stupendous waterfall cascading from an unbelievable height between the mountains. It was Sutherland's turn. "Now Mackay," Donald could well have said. "We are not tossing a coin for this one."

Its silent stately magnificence, brought to perfection by the distant view, held its discoverers in thrall. But they were practical men and as their food supplies were exhausted, they resisted the temptation to cover the last two remaining miles to the foot of the falls and turned their steps homeward.

With this discovery on 10 November 1880 another solid link was forged in the chain of events which brought to life the world-famed Milford Track. In their pardonable enthusiasm the falls grew in their imagination till their estimated height was declared to be 4,000, perhaps 5,000 feet. Donald Sutherland was well-known for his ability to add refinements to a good story. He knew very well, of course, that the height would add up to a much less fantastic figure. He could make a rough estimate of the height they had reached above sea level, and with the bushline to guide him could, better than many another man, come near to the right answer.

Naturally the news of their discovery stirred fresh interest in that region. The vision of a railroad had never grown dim and now, with the supposedly highest waterfall in the world to exploit, there was additional support for this idea. A small party was sent from Invercargill by Superintendent James Macandrew to make an exploratory survey of the Milford Sound region. They were John Robinson, surveyor, W. Y. H. Hall, solicitor, and S. H. Moreton, artist. They covered much of the ground explored by Sir James Hector and others and, like them, had to report that no feasible route for a railway could be found.

Sutherland took the party up the Arthur River to Lake Ada. They followed the right bank Moreton described as a boulder track, the boulders varying in size from a hatbox to a house. Alternating from the boulders to the bush they found their way to the foot of the lake where they camped for the night.

Their guide then introduced them to his canoe, a seventeen-foot job, dug out of a big beech tree and taking four days to fashion into a useful craft. They paddled up the lake and were captivated by the scenery, more particularly by the Terror Mountains with the great cleft of Giant's Gate on the saddle below them.

Robinson and Hall returned to Invercargill but Moreton remained and subsequently sketched all round the lake and up Jose River (as he spelt Joe's River). The scenery up Joe's Valley was magnificent, but he was convinced there was no passage to be found to the interior by that way.

Some three or four years previously, Sutherland and Mackay, at the instance of the Lake County, had endeavoured to find a pass that would lead to Lake Wakatipu, and after fruitless searching up the Cleddau and its tributaries they had turned their attention to

31

the Arthur Valley and investigated Joe's Valley. Signs of their camp were still to be seen at the head of the lake.

They would have been quite familiar with this region before they explored the upper reaches which had led them to discover the famous waterfall. Some writers assume they went on foot round the lake but in the light of their earlier activities this seems unlikely. We have good grounds for believing the lake was first explored from its waters rather than from its shores. Sutherland's interest was first in its eastern side and he would see and name the Giant's Gate before he knew of the waterfall, which when discovered naturally acquired the same name. A perpendicular bluff at the lower end on the eastern side, and another at the head on the western, while not impossible barriers, would in normal circumstances be avoided. Obstacles such as these would appear no more inviting to Sutherland and Mackay than they did to McKenzie and Pillans when they launched their crazy canvas boat, or to Richard Henry when he preferred his corrugated iron contraption to bring him down the lake in 1889.

In a letter to Mr W. Boers, Samuel Moreton describes a visit to the Sutherland Falls during this sojourn at Milford. This does not square with what C. W. Adams has to say, for according to his account the falls were not seen for the second time till 1883 when Sutherland, Hart and Moreton reached a point about a mile distant. Another account states that John Mackay also accompanied the party. Thomas McKenzie also relates that when he and Pillans, accompanied by Sutherland, reached the base of the falls in 1888 they were told by the discoverer that they were first to have done so.

Moreton's letter, written years after the event, may have omitted what appeared to be irrelevant detail and did in fact describe the 1883 visit, but he does not mention any companion other than Donald Sutherland.

His letter records that setting out for the falls, they spent the first night camped at the foot of the lake. On the second night they camped about a mile up the river beyond the lake where they found signs of Maori occupation at a comparatively recent date. In looking over the ground, they came across the Maoris' futta pole (food store) and further on, patches of nettles, which as an article of diet never fail to attract the Maori. Their presence here confirmed the early claim that they were familiar with the way through from Te Anau to Milford.

ABOVE: The Quintin Huts
in early 1900.

RIGHT: The Te Anau Hotel
in 1915.

BELOW: The first Glade
House built in 1895.

ABOVE: Mid Hut in the Clinton Valley, 1901.

RIGHT: The Government Hut at the mouth of the Clinton River. Built in 1890, it was used by tourists until 1896, when the first Glade House was opened adjacent to the present building.

Quintin MacKinnon (*seated*) accompanied by Ernest Mitchell discovered the MacKinnon Pass in 1888.

It may be that Kupa Haeroroa's invasion in 1872 gave the local Maoris the hint that their domain was no longer a sanctuary and persuaded them to withdraw further into the wilds.

Moreton describes the journey up to the falls as exceedingly rough. From their riverside camp it took them a full day to reach the shingle beach where Roaring Creek enters the Arthur River. Here they camped and on the next day proceeded up to the falls. Their first view of Mt Balloon filled them with amazement. Moreton described it as a great horn rising an estimated 3,000 feet in height above the range. The range itself (now known as MacKinnon Pass) appeared to be about 3,750 feet. This is remarkably close to its actual height. Moreton records that Sutherland named the mountain but does not give his reason. Superimposed, as it were, on the range it could have suggested a detached entity like a balloon. The first glimpse they would get would be the cone appearing over the spur of Mt Elliot from which angle the likeness to a balloon is very marked. Mr Hart was the first person to photograph the Sutherland Falls and his name was given to the mountain between the falls and Mt Balloon.

Samuel Moreton's paintings and his description of the scenic grandeur of the Arthur Valley added weight to earlier reports and helped to move the various interested authorities to exploit its scenic and other potentialities.

During the next few years rewards were offered for the discovery of a practical route to Milford by the Otago and Southland Provincial authorities. The Government also offered a £50 reward. £300, a princely sum in those days, was offered by the Wallace County Council. Encouragement of this nature was not, however, matched by positive action till in 1888 a strong survey party, with C. W. Adams, Chief Surveyor of Otago in charge, was dispatched to Milford Sound to survey the head of the Sound, Arthur Valley, measure the height of the Sutherland Falls and endeavour to find a practical route to the interior.

To further the latter project it was arranged that Quintin MacKinnon should investigate the Clinton Valley to try and find a pass while the main party were similarly engaged on the Milford side.

The party left Bluff on 26 September in the *Ohau* and arrived at Milford Sound the following afternoon. On the same day they landed stores and W. S. Pillans liberated some trout fry in the Cleddau River. The following day while Mr Adams and his men

33

were still engaged at the sound, McKenzie, Pillans, Muir and others set off for Lake Ada taking with them provisions and materials with which to make a canvas boat.

The next day at 3 pm they launched their craft, described by McKenzie as "a crank affair" and with their baggage and a dog, pushed off on their perilous trip up the lake. A breeze ruffled the surface of the lake and obscured the treacherous sharp-toothed tree trunks with which the lake was studded, contact with which could easily mean disaster. With night coming on they pulled ashore and camped some two miles up the river beyond the lake. Up early the next morning, they continued on up the river where Pillans liberated another thousand trout fry. Leaving their companions to return to camp, McKenzie and Pillans landed and made their way up the valley. Some miles on they came up with Donald Sutherland, who accompanied them to the Sutherland Falls.

T. McKenzie relates that Donald Sutherland marked the occasion by naming the mountain to the right of the falls McKenzie, and the one directly across the valley Pillans. Donald Sutherland, it seems, was expected to have the track cut up to the falls and a hut built in a suitable place near the head of the valley in readiness for the arrival of the survey party. No doubt this is what had taken him up there at this time. McKenzie, Pillans and Sutherland went back to Milford and another member, Wyinks, returned with them to continue the exploration of the upper Arthur Valley.

They first went up Joe's River where Sam Moreton had made his lone exploratory and sketching excursion some five or six years before, satisfied, as he was, that there was no right-of-way in that direction.

Next they turned their attention to Staircase Creek with no greater success. They named the waterfall a mile or so up Staircase Creek (seen from the track near the Sutherland Falls) the Heron Falls. Famished and weary after their prolonged exertions they retraced their footsteps in the direction of their base camp, intending to return and investigate Roaring Creek.

While they had been thus engaged Mr Adams and some of his men came up from Milford and measured the height of the Sutherland Falls, finding them 1,904 feet, the top leap 815, the middle 751 and the lower 338 feet.

One of Adams' men remarked that he saw "four explorers" coming over the pass near Mt Balloon. They were black swans which he said would cross the mountains at their lowest point. He remarked that he wouldn't be surprised if this proved to be the pass they were looking for. Those who believe that coming events cast their shadows would see in this flight a portent of the great event to follow. Before we investigate, however, we should take a look at what has been going on across the mountains.

Quintin MacKinnon and Ernest Mitchell had left Manapouri on 2 September 1888 with the Clinton Valley as their destination. They called at Lynwood Station where they stayed the night, going on to Mellands' at Te Anau Downs the following day. After two days' enforced stay owing to bad weather, they set off by boat for the head of the lake on the seventh, taking with them tents, tools and provisions. They reached a mile up the river before disembarking and setting up camp.

Ernest Mitchell of Manapouri Station was a powerfully-built, steady, reliable young fellow, a splendid right-hand man for the redoubtable Quintin MacKinnon. All their strength, endurance, patience and determination were to be severely tested in the next two months.

Quintin MacKinnon was born in the Shetland Islands. Like Sutherland, his adventurous spirit led him at an early age to go abroad and take part in another country's war and for a time he fought on the side of the French in the Franco-Prussian War. On arrival in New Zealand, he followed his profession as a surveyor but, seeking greater freedom to satisfy his roving instincts, he became a freelance, and with Te Anau as his headquarters made frequent excursions into the unknown territory surrounding it. When the survey party went round to Milford Sound he was only too eager to supplement their efforts to find the long-sought-for key which would open the door to that enchanted land.

On 17 September they started to cut the track. On that same day they caught a rabbit, the first they had seen there. It seems remarkable that rabbits should be found there at that early time. They don't readily go far into dense bush, and they would have many miles of it to traverse before reaching the open glades in the Clinton Valley.

For the next three weeks the pathfinders continued their arduous labours, enduring all the misery the elements in that region could heap upon them. One very hot and sultry day gave them a very unpleasant surprise when they returned to camp to find their blankets one moving mass of blowflies. Heavy rain found its way into their tents until it was as wet inside as out. Working and sleeping in wet clothes gave them sores which hampered them in their work and interfered with their hours of rest. Food ran short and they were reduced to one meal a day. Thunderstorms with terrific lightning found them shivering in their tents, unable to get a fire going to make a hot drink, dry their clothes and bedding or drive out the cold which had soaked right into them. On 28 September they came to a lake. From their description it would be what is now called Hidden Lake, where a loop track allowing it to be seen now leaves the main track to rejoin it a quarter of a mile farther on.

On 6 October they retreated to their first camp and found the river had risen twelve feet in their absence, ruining all the stores they had left there, making them return to Te Anau Downs to replenish them. On the seventh they sailed their boat down to Mellands' station at the Downs, their sails torn to ribbons and themselves drenched by the driving spray.

They were given dry clothes, a luxury they had not enjoyed for a week. They had a good night's sleep in a dry bed, but enticing as it must have been to have remained longer to recuperate, they started off back the next day. They reached Safe Cove that night and camped there, completing their journey the next morning. Pulling their boat up to a safe distance from the water's edge they set off to the forward camp, nine miles distant, very heavily laden with supplies. This trip took seven and a half hours.

Slogging away for the next few days, hindered only by the inevitable rain, they dropped their tools and went forward to see what the country was like, and now, feeling more confident, they decided they would do no more cutting but make a dash for it over the pass. Leaving the camp early the next morning, they found a little way beyond the point they had reached the day before, a little lake they named Lake Beautiful. MacKinnon later renamed it Mintaro. What prompted him to bestow this name on the lake is a mystery. There is a township, Mintaro, in South Australia, named it is popularly believed by the Spanish muleteers who ran mule trains and bullock waggons between the coast and copper mines at Burra, about 100 miles inland. Mintaro marked one of their stages where there was water for their teams. In Spanish it means resting place.

We have not been able to discover if MacKinnon had any connection with or knowledge of the township in Australia, but it seems more than a coincidence that he would use a name so rare and at the same time so descriptive of the place. For, it must be remembered, this, not Pompolona, was the resting place at the beginning between Lake Te Anau and the Sutherland Falls.

Right up against the pass they determined that, whatever lay on the other side, nothing would stop them now. Making use of every handhold and foothold they dragged themselves up to the top. Had the day been fine and clear they would have been better able to appraise the situation but with poor visibility, pelted by stinging wind-driven raindrops, they could only grope their way along the pass looking for a possible way down. This they did not find until they reached the base of Mt Balloon. With night coming on, they halted at the first reasonable shelter they could find, some distance down from the top. With everything dripping wet it was impossible to light a fire so they went to bed supperless.

In the morning the prospect was no better so they cut out breakfast as well, scrambled down to the bushline and on until at 2 pm they came on to a shingle beach where there was some dry wood. They raised a fire and served themselves a good dinner of grilled blue mountain duck. Going on farther they intercepted Donald Sutherland's track and then they knew for certain they had accomplished what they had set themselves to do.

They left a message written on a card with the date of their arrival addressed to Mr Sutherland or Mr Adams, saying that they were going on down the river. They camped some three miles on and the next day went on, as they say, to the lake, but probably it was only as far as the lagoon now known as Lake Brown. They returned to their camp, spent another wet day there, then on the following day, just as they were ready to eat a good meal they had just prepared, some visitors arrived.

The visitors' dog, first on the scene as is the way with dogs, announced their coming. Thinking of the only likely person to be found there, Quintin called out from inside, "Hallo Sutherland."

Wyinks had known MacKinnon well and recognised his voice. "Hallo Mac," he returned.

MacKinnon, muttering about someone making himself very familiar, came with the others into view, and on recognition, hailed the newcomers with jubilation and an invitation to tuck in to his meal. The half-starved visitors were Wyinks, Pillans and McKenzie who had come upon MacKinnon's message on their way down from their exploration of the Arthur River.

The next day MacKinnon, Wyinks and Mitchell put together the canvas boat and, with one oar partnered by a makeshift apology for the other, they took the rapids in their stride and arrived safely at the foot of the lake.

MacKinnon made his report to the Chief Surveyor, then, leaving Mitchell to wait at Milford for the coming ship, he rejoined McKenzie and Pillans and with Muir (photographer) returned over the newly-found pass to Te Anau. In a snowstorm they found it not so easy making their way up and over the pass, and it was with great thankfulness they reached the comparative safety of the Clinton. The cold here was less intense but the going exceedingly tough until they reached the head of the track which led to the old camp.

The next day they reached the spot where the boat had been left and pushed off immediately at about 3 pm. It was still stormy and when night came on they ran aground. They got off again but only the skill of MacKinnon saved them from swamping in the turbulent waters. They finally arrived at Lumsden where Mac-Kinnon sent a telegram to Wellington acquainting the Government with the discovery of the long-sought-for highway to Milford.

4

THE MILFORD TRACK TAKES SHAPE

THE NEWS THAT AN OPEN WAY had been found to Milford Sound was hailed with delight and satisfaction by the country at large and Southland in particular.

One who did not overwhelm MacKinnon with congratulations was Donald Sutherland. Decidedly ruffled that he was not the discoverer of the pass to which he had been so close for eight years, he is said to have retorted dourly that "he could have found the track at any time if he'd wanted to do so". He refused to call the pass by its discoverer's name, persisting in speaking of it as Balloon Saddle.

This further instance of Sutherland's dourness is but another side of a singular man. He certainly was unusual, both in appearance and manner. Tall, broad, sternfaced, with light brown beard and searching blue eyes, he was reticent, and at times truculent to the point of being described by some as eccentric. Certainly his abrupt speech and distaste for city dwellers, whom he bitingly described as *Asphalters*, did not easily win him friends, especially as he regarded Milford very much as his own. His feuds have become remarkable, preserved in his Visitors' Book, but towards his friends he exhibited a generous friendliness.

He was not really a recluse, nor completely averse to company. For the increasing number of tourists who started to arrive at Milford he organised entertainment in the form of various races and sold them birds which he had stuffed. Considerate guests found him helpful and agreeable. To those who were otherwise Sutherland was brusque indeed.

Otago people experienced a shade of disappointment that a more direct route had not been found to serve their province. The main drive to find a link with Milford had been made via Wakatipu and the Hollyford Valley, and in spite of the discovery of the Mackinnon Pass, the notion still persisted that a more serviceable route could still be found. At about this time W. H. Homer, who had narrowed down the search to the head of the Hollyford, strongly advocated the construction of a tunnel linking the Hollyford and Cleddau valleys. More than fifty years were to elapse before his recommendation was acted upon and the tunnel became a reality. Not till 1910 was a path found over the mountains and then a far from satisfactory one. This was by way of the Gertrude Saddle. Its discoverers were the veteran mountaineers Grave and Talbot. Until the tunnel was opened it had a limited use and some Milford Track walkers went over it instead of retracing their steps to Te Anau by the way they had come.

A progressive policy of development instituted by the Government now assured the future of the Track. The services of the survey party were retained to continue the good work begun so auspiciously.

Donald Sutherland finished his contract of cutting a track to the "Falls" and putting up a hut at Roaring Creek. Quintin MacKinnon was similarly engaged on his end of the track.

In November 1888 Mr McKerrow, Surveyor-General, visiting Dunedin, stated that it was planned to put a boat on Lake Ada and improve the track to the falls, both from Te Anau and Milford. By the next summer he expected it would be in good enough condition for ladies to use. The first lady to walk the whole length of the track was Mrs Samuel Moreton. Accompanied by her husband, it took them two days in a boat rowing up Lake Te Anau to reach its head, two more days to reach Mintaro, ten hours to cross the saddle and reach Beech Hut. On the sixth day she completed the journey to Milford, arriving on 7 February 1890.

C. W. Adams' map from his first survey makes an interesting comparison with the Track as we know it today. Beginning from Sandfly Point, the Track originally followed up the right bank of the Arthur River to Lake Ada. Then, to avoid the rapids in the river above the lake, the surveyors frequently used Lake Brown from which they made a track to the Upper Landing (now Boatshed). At the bluff below Boatshed they had a makeshift arrangement of saplings to enable them to negotiate it and later a track was blasted out of the rock. Roaring Creek was forded at the present horse-crossing and Quintin MacKinnon's track, beginning near Quintin, kept to the same side of Roaring Creek and Moraine Creek. The track took a lower course than the present one from the bushline up to the pass, and it went round

Lake Ella on its western side instead of some distance to the east where the huts are located.

The surveyors returned the next season on 15 October 1889, coming from Bluff in the government steamer *Hinemoa*. After unloading the stores and tools, they lost no time in starting with the work on the track. They now turned their attention to the left bank of the Arthur River which, although more rocky, rough and less attractive than the other, gave better access to the western side of Lake Ada where the track would be formed. They built a hut at Doughboy, the landing place at the foot of Lake Ada, and improved the track enough for them to carry the heavier and more awkward loads over it.

William Quill, from whose diary we learn much of their exploits, carried a hundred-pound barrel of salt beef plus the gallon of brine it contained and the weight of the barrel itself, an estimated 140 pounds in all. It took him four hours to carry it the two miles from Sandfly Point to Doughboy. Everything had to be carried on their backs and loads up to 100 pounds were not uncommon. After a fortnight of trackmaking and packing stores, they moved up to Poseidon Hut, now suffering the plain name of Boatshed. Donald Sutherland named the upper Arthur River, Poseidon, and the hut not unnaturally acquired that name.

While most of his companions were engaged in trackmaking William Quill was given the responsible task of building another boat. In a few days it was completed and at the launching was christened the *Lizzie* by Mr Adams with a pannikin of hot tea.

The next camp was set up three miles distant from Poseidon Hut where the river below the rapids leaves the track to make a wide sweep before closing in on it again at Diamond Creek, three-quarters of a mile from the hut.

With the hopes of supplying this camp by the river an investigation was made with the flattie manned by Mr Adams, Quill and W. Coutts. Quill describes it as a "wicked place to take a load up but great fun coming down shooting the rapids". A few days later he and Coutts took (to quote his diary) "the first boat of stuff that has ever been taken as far as the slip". The slip he mentions was a large one, which, combined with an avalanche from the western slope of Mt Elliot, obliterated the track. The camp set up there was known as Slip Camp. Traces of that old camp are still to be seen there.

41

Quill and Coutts shifted up to Slip Camp while other members of the party went up to Bunger Hut (as Quill called it). This was the hut recently put up by Donald Sutherland. Mr Adams chose a new site where the "Beech Hut" was erected and later shifted Donald's hut from the bank of Roaring Creek and re-erected it alongside the other.

Work went on clearing the slip, interrupted by the shipping of another boatload of stores from Poseidon Hut and a number of days of pouring rain. The final boatload was taken up on the day before Christmas. Their tussle with the river and the elements is best told in Quill's own words.

"After getting all aboard we left at 11.15 am. The several rapids were running at full force and seemed to grin at our efforts as we dragged our heavy load, sometimes by sheer strength until we pushed it into some benevolent eddy, thereby cheating the unmanageable influence of the growing current, accumulating every moment by the increasing rain that was pouring down in torrents, leaving us drenched to the skin until the rain and wet could penetrate no further. Got everything up safe and dry owing no doubt to our oilskins with which we had covered the load. (At 3.15, four hours' time through a dozen rapids and swollen river.)"

The rain on Christmas Eve continued over Christmas Day and until noon on Boxing Day. The dull monotony of these frequent periods of rain, in cramped uncomfortable quarters, are remarked upon by William Quill, but youth, abounding energy, with interest and zest in the life and work, quickly shed depression when at last the skies cleared. After heavy rain, one is frequently well repaid by the crystal clearness of the atmosphere which brings the mountain tops into sharp relief, turns the sky a deeper blue, the ferns, mosses and forest leaves a brighter, richer green.

With the completion of the work at the slip, the track improved between it and Boatshed, and, the last of the stores brought up, Quill and his companions left Slip Camp to join the others up at Beech Hut on 28 December. The following day Mr Morgan and Jack Quill, William's brother, came over from Te Anau. Mr Morgan was in charge of the party which started work at the beginning of December to improve the track on that side of the pass.

Sunday was the only day off from work and, as most of the Sundays were wet, there was little opportunity of seeing anything beyond the place where they were working, but there was the occasional visit to the Sound for mail and additional stores, which arrived at irregular intervals by various vessels. From Poseidon Hut, Quill and some of the others had made their first visit to the Sutherland Falls, and now, Sunday 5 January dawning a beautiful day, Quill and Ted Wilkins went up again to the falls. On this occasion the former wanted to have a closer look at the possibility of climbing the cliff-face alongside the falls. He and Ted climbed to the top of the second leap where they planted a flag they had taken with them, feeling confident they would reach that far. On the following day Quill enters in his diary: "Beautiful day. Clearing bush and trees and levelling site for new or old Beech Hut." The hut referred to is the one Donald Sutherland had built which now had to be shifted to the new site. The site for Beech Hut was chosen to place it in more direct line with Sutherland Falls when approaching from the Pass, and to reduce the grade on the last steep portion of the track.

Work went steadily on at the huts, and on the tracks which radiated from them. Occasional parties from the Sound came up to visit the Sutherland Falls, and others came from Te Anau, to do the same, a few going on down to Milford. On rare occasions Donald Sutherland would accompany a party from Milford, and more frequently Quintin MacKinnon from Te Anau.

All was not plain sailing with the stores. William Quill records that once, after they had been out of beef for ten days and potatoes for as many weeks, he went down when the SS *Tarawera* was expected, to get supplies. On that occasion the barrel of beef he carried up to Doughboy weighed only seventy pounds, and it took him only an hour. He returned and went for another load, sixty pounds of potatoes. After the heavy swagging, they enjoyed the luxury of the trip up the lake, the boat, driven by a following wind with a bed-quilt for sail, carrying them well into the river above the lake in forty-five minutes.

During the month of February 1890, William Quill made his first visit to the MacKinnon Pass, finding it in his own words, "not half as bad as some make it out to be". On the seventh, while engaged in carrying stores to Doughboy he met Samuel Moreton and his wife on their way to the Sound, the first lady, he says, to have come over the saddle (MacKinnon Pass).

This feat is substantiated by Mrs Moreton's own glowing entry in Sutherland's guidebook: "Arrived from Te Anau. Delighted with my trip as I am the *first lady* to have crossed from Te Anau to Milford."

For Moreton, artist and explorer, this was one of the many times he returned to his beloved Milford after he had left the locality in 1883. He was one of the earliest of Sutherland's companions, being, after Sutherland and Mackay, one of the first men to view the Sutherland Falls. Moreton spent from 1881 to 1883 at Milford, and he also assisted in improving the blazed trail up the valley of the Arthur. He had a kind of working partnership with Sutherland in his accommodation venture. He had, as well, accompanied Sutherland in the first attempted ascent of Mitre Peak.

Moreton departed for Christchurch where he set up an art school. In the tea break from classes he dearly loved recounting to his pupils his explorations in the then unknown Fiordland. Apart from his frequent visits to Fiordland, he and his wife made painting and exploring trips into the headwaters of the Rakaia and Lake Heron district. One of his pupils, Arthur A. F. Winder, has told me of his own excursion to Lake Heron after the artist's death in 1922 to bring out his camping equipment for Mrs Moreton.

The ninth of March 1890 proved a red letter day for William Quill for on that beautiful autumn day he climbed the face of the Sutherland Falls, a feat in itself to give the greatest satisfaction, without in addition the discovery of a lake, a jewel set among the mountains and the fount of the famous waterfall. His remarkable achievement he accomplished in two and a half hours in ascending and the same in coming down.

The veteran explorers Donald Sutherland and Samuel Moreton arrived the next day, accompanying Mrs Moreton on her way back over the track. William Quill would receive hearty congratulations and they would appreciate to the full his prowess and achievement.

The following Sunday being fine, Quill again ascended the falls, this time taking three and a half hours to go up and one and a half to come down. This time he crossed the stream above the falls and climbed Mt Sutherland (now McKenzie).

On Sunday 4 May William Quill, this time taking with him Bill Coutts, climbed the falls for the third time, but instead of returning the same way went back over Mt Hart. "There is a splendid view all around," he says, "including that of the briny."

Late in March the Chief Surveyor of Otago, C. W. Adams, arrived at Milford by the *Tarawera*. He was accompanied by his eleven-year-old daughter, Ella, who has left an interesting account of her walk over the Milford Track. He had arranged to be met at the Sound by some members of the survey party. They, however, had been held up by rain, and Donald Sutherland was away. As they were put ashore, the passengers pitied the lonely pair in their isolation and persuaded the captain to give them food to take ashore with them. Ella felt the loneliness of their position and the overpowering influence of the high mountains which hemmed them in and seemed to tower threateningly over them. Fortunately for her peace of mind, she did not know how worried her father was at the non-arrival of the party. They retired early and in the early hours of the morning they heard a cooee from across the river. The Cleddau at that time flowed close past the point on which Milford was built and they crossed it in their little canvas boat.

On the same day they started off on their way to Beech Huts. They crossed Lake Ada in the canvas boat. This seems strange as at that time they had at least three boats on Lake Ada, all in good condition. Mr Adams (usually supposed to be the Chief Surveyor's son, but he seems more likely to have been his brother) and Wilkins met them at the Sound and returned with them, while Quill and Coutts met them with the *Blue Boat* at the lower rapids at the lagoon (Lake Brown). The weather was bad and they did not get away from the Beech Huts till 5 April, five days later. Ella paid the falls a visit while at Beech Huts. With the heavy rains the falls were putting on a great display, the spray driving heavily down the track from their base.

The Beech Huts were crudely built with rough slabs for walls which did not keep out the great numbers of bush rats. Ella was not afraid of them but did not like them running all over her as soon as the lights went out, so she begged some calico from her father to make a head covering. She made holes in it so that she could breathe and that way she felt much happier. The huts had pretty curtains on the windows and, wondering where they came from, she was told a fantasy by one of the survey party that they came from the dress of a French countess who had made a trip up to the falls. The track in its primitive state left the countess minus shoes and with only the lining of her dress.

45

Ella and her father went over the Pass accompanied by Quintin MacKinnon and her uncle, while three of the surveyors, Quill, Wilkins and Coutts, went ahead with the packs and got the camp ready at Mintaro. They met Mr Morgan on the Pass, who took Wilkins' pack, allowing him to return to Beech Huts. At one steep slippery place Ella was roped to Quintin MacKinnon. On the top they passed a little tarn which was given the name Ella in her honour.

The creek at Pompolona was running a good deal of water and Ella was carried over it by Jack Quill. The farther down the valley they went the easier she found the walking and the Clinton River, as it never fails to do, charmed her with its clear greenish waters.

On the lake the weather was perfectly calm and it took three days rowing to reach the station at the Downs. They camped two nights on the shore, one on the west side, the other on the east. They went on horseback to Lumsden and from there by rail home to Dunedin.

The parties both in the Arthur and Clinton valleys carried on their work until late in May. Looking back on their season's toil they could feel justly proud of their accomplishments. They had turned the blazed tracks into a serviceable (much of it easy) walking path from one end to the other. They had erected huts at strategic positions along the way. Creeks had been bridged and made safe in all but the flood rains which, in any case, suspend all normal traffic. The Track was now really open for business.

Donald Sutherland was able to attend to the excursionists coming by sea. Quintin MacKinnon was in command of the situation from Te Anau. The trickle of sightseers already started would by their enthusiastic advertisement of the Track's scenic qualities cause that trickle to grow to an ever-swelling stream.

The closing days of the season brought harsher conditions for the track-makers. The sun more briefly appeared above the mountain tops, the rains were cold with snow creeping down nearer to the valleys. The supply of rations became more erratic. The larder had to be supplemented more and more with native game. With the end in sight, thoughts of home would allow less patience with adverse conditions. Nevertheless Quill's entry on the day he left shows no such reactions.

On Monday 26 May 1890 he writes: "Beautiful day. Left West Coast at last and with regret. SS *Te Uira* departed the head of the lake at 8 am, reached foot 5 pm, nine hours steaming. A pleasant voyage down the lake. Stopped at new Lake Hotel and found it excellent in every respect."

Unfortunately this intelligent observant young man was not to work for much longer in Fiordland. Early in the following year he and his two younger brothers, sons of Mr T. Quill, Kuri Bush, Taieri, were members of the survey parties, under the charge of Mr Simpson and Mr Ross, who were searching for a tourist route from Wakatipu to Milford Sound.

While it was known that one, if not two saddles overlooked the Cleddau Valley in Milford, one, the Homer, had a sheer western face. With the idea of exploring the feasibility of putting a short tunnel through the razorback emerging in the valley at the foot of the precipice, Quill and Simpson went round by Te Anau and over the MacKinnon Pass into Milford. From here they went up the Cleddau, only to be confronted with the difficulty that, among all the precipitous faces, they could not select that of Homer's Saddle.

There was nothing for it but to return to the Wakatipu side and mark the location in some way. On 12 January, Quill started from the Greenstone Camp to place a flag and cairn on the summit of the Pass so that it could be seen from the Milford side. This he did. He was offered a companion, but declined, saying there was no need of one. He set out alone for Homer's Saddle and, after placing the flag-topped cairn on its summit, he returned to his camp where he left a message that he was going to try and reach the Cleddau by way of Gertrude Saddle, three miles to the north. His intended route was left in his diary and also in a memo written on a piece of a paper bag. "Gone to Gertrude Saddle and trying to get down to Cleddau Valley. Will Quill Jan 15, '91, 7 am."

It was his last note. On his non-return, his brother and two others made for Gertrude Saddle to search for him.

They crossed it and reached a point 900 feet below the saddle on the western side to be stopped by a precipice. Just above it they noticed a tuft of grass wrenched from the ground as if by a man's heel. This evidence plus a footprint they had found earlier, 500 feet down, convinced them that Quill had fallen over the precipice.

Descent from such a place being unthinkable, they returned to Greenstone. They hoped from the Milford side to be able to single out the point of Quill's fall and to find him at the bottom. His body was never found.

So died one of Fiordland's most enthusiastic explorers and climbers. He was only twenty-five years old, but has left his mark on the steep country he explored. The sheet of water which he was the first to see and from which the wonderful Sutherland Falls are fed is named Lake Quill.

Donald Sutherland (*left*) in 1915.

RIGHT: SS *Tawera* in 1901. Captain Murray-Menzies is at the wheel.

BELOW: Early days in the construction of the Homer Tunnel in the Hollyford Valley.

Toot Carran's garden seat. (*Bac
row*) Brian Blackie, Dorothy Cald
well, Arthur Anderson, and two
trampers. (*Front row*) Nick Haggi
Mrs May Anderson, Bill Anderso
and Julia Stevens (née Anderson).

ABOVE: Samuel Moreton and C. White-
Parsons in 1901.

RIGHT: *From left*, May Anderson,
Arthur Anderson and Dorothy Caldwell.

BELOW: Quintin MacKinnon's Two
Mile Hut in the Clinton Valley in
1901. This photograph was taken on
the day that Queen Victoria died.

5

MILFORD AND TE ANAU AWAKEN

BEFORE THE DISCOVERY of the MacKinnon Pass, Te Anau slumbered on the edge of the unknown. Now, with pleased surprise, it awakened to find itself on the highway to Milford. Having proclaimed a lively faith in its future before this event, even its most vocal prophets were taken unawares and caught up in the overflowing flood of actual fulfilment of their prophecies.

The interest shown by the Government, endorsed by a vigorous effort to exploit this discovery, was enough to awaken the latent forces of private enterprise.

This tiny community of less than a dozen souls, isolated by many miles of shocking roads and cut off from the outside world by lack of telephone service, braced itself for the day when its resources would be taxed to provide hospitality for a swelling stream of visitors.

Richard Henry, caretaker of Resolution Island, 1894-1909, was the first settler at Te Anau and is also remembered as the discoverer of the route to George Sound. Australian born, he arrived at Te Anau from Marlborough in 1883 and built the first hut at the south end of the lake. For the next ten years he stayed there doing odd jobs for runholders and exploring the surrounding country. In 1899, with Robert Murrell of Manapouri, he made the first crossing of Henry Saddle to reach George Sound. In 1889, following in MacKinnon's footsteps, he became the second person to cross the Milford Track.

With the object of preserving our native birds, he was in 1894 made caretaker of Resolution Island. The remains of the two-roomed house he built on Pigeon Island can still be seen today. For the next fourteen years he took some 400 kakapo as well as other flightless birds to the safety of the islands in Dusky Sound. This venture nearly ended in 1900 when he found one stoat on Resolution Island, and others actually swimming the two miles from

49

the mainland. From 1909 to 1911 he lived as custodian on Kapiti Island. He died in 1929.

In 1888-89, during the first season the Track was opened, some forty visitors reached the Sutherland Falls; the next season, seventy, and during 1890-91, about one hundred. This was not a great number to cater for or to build hopes upon, but the people of Te Anau were confident that the three figures would soon grow to four.

Captain Brodrick, applying his skill acquired as a ship's carpenter, with his broad-axe fashioned all the timbers for his eight-roomed accommodation house, situated where the post office now stands. Captain Duncan, artist, with his sister at his "Bush Studio", also provided accommodation, and with the opening of the hotel, built by William Snodgrass, "Marakura", as it was then known, was in a position to welcome all comers. John McKenzie, described as the "Prince of Coachmen", with his four-horse coach conducted his passengers safely over next to impassable roads and at times flooded streams. Each of the residents owned a boat, powered by sail and oar, available for service on the lake.

The excursions to the head of the lake, lengthy in terms of miles and time, could supply many surprises and dangers. One party in the eighties, depending on the use of Captain Brodrick's whaleboat, found it had met with misadventure and had broken up. They had to be content with a flattie, fortunately well-built, of Richard Henry's workmanship, which they rowed to the head of the lake. After exploring some distance up the Worsley River, they returned to their camp at the lakeside. A terrible storm arose and in the dead of a pitch-black night, rising waters forced them to embark. By a miracle they kept afloat and eventually found their way to safety. The longest trip recorded was one taken by Quintin Mac-Kinnon, who, with a photographer, made a complete circuit of the lake, a three-month job.

Presently two small steamers appeared on the lake, the *Ripple* and *Te Uira*. Steaming flat-out these models could reach the head of the lake in ten or twelve hours; nothing in the performance to get excited about, but an improvement on the erratic time made by their sail and oar competitors. Unimpressed by its performance, same wag dared to paint the letter "C" before the name *Ripple* on the side of the steamer. Wondering what was amusing some idlers at the wharf, Captain Brodrick's reaction was very different from theirs when he found the reason. The offending letter was promptly erased, but the vessel's reputation suffered a "crippling" blow from which it never recovered, for it was known for the rest of its life as *The Cripple*. Later, it seems, it was acquired by William Snodgrass.

Te Uira escaped more lightly than the *Ripple*, for her name, interpreted by the bush etymologists, was rendered "Greased Lightning".

At different times Captain Brodrick skippered both these steamers. Brod's Bay, across the lake from the township, perpetuates his name. There he loaded firewood to fuel his boilers and, trading on the anxiety of his passengers to get under way, he would stall until in their own interests they would set to and get the wood on board.

Robust characters such as "Brod" are usually to be found in primitive communities, but Te Anau was fortunate in being pioneered by men who, while lacking nothing in rugged qualities, were gentlemen at heart.

Supplemented by government grants, the Wallace County steadily pushed forward road construction, but many years were to elapse before the township was served with well-surfaced roads and telephonic communication.

While the Te Anau residents were coming to grips with demanding situations, Donald Sutherland, on the other side of the mountains, was not idle. During the interval between the departure of the surveyors and the coming of the next season's workers, Donald paid Dunedin a visit. While there he married thrice-widowed Elizabeth Samuel. Born in England, Elizabeth Bull had at the age of seventeen married a Greek, named Cossum. After his death she married an American, Donald McKenzie, and they both emigrated to New Zealand. McKenzie died in 1871, and the following year brought her marriage to Joseph Samuel. Ten years later she was again a widow, and by the time of her marriage to Donald Sutherland on 7 August 1890 she was a grandmother.

Her final marriage was a great partnership. She spent the rest of her life at Milford, a devoted wife to Sutherland, and soon became known for her hospitality to travellers. Her initiative, money and experience were now directed towards life at the Sound. They had been married only six months when Donald made over to her his "City of Milford" by deed for £100, and five acres of land for the building of a guesthouse.

Work was begun on a ten-roomed house, followed by two cottages and other buildings. They were now able to cater for visitors arriving by sea, and also coming over the Track from Te Anau.

Quintin MacKinnon had his establishment at Garden Point at the entrance to the South Fiord of Lake Te Anau. He had here first two tents, and later a hut. He would bring his parties from the Te Anau coach terminus by his whaleboat, *Juliet*, to the head of the lake. Then he would escort them over the Track, and Mac-Kinnon Pass, by boat across Lake Ada and the Sound, to Mrs Sutherland's chalet at Milford.

The good work accomplished by the survey men in opening up the Track and the glowing accounts of all who visited the Sutherland Falls, encouraged the Government to embark on an ambitious plan to build a road from Milford Sound to the falls. Eventually it would go right through to the head of Lake Te Anau. This carriageway, as it was called, was to be a magnificent highway twenty-five feet wide.

With the object, no doubt, of keeping the financial cost to a reasonable figure, it was proposed to use prison labour. A working gang of forty-five was sent to Milford Sound in the government steamer *Hinemoa*. Alexander Hulme, Inspector of Prisons, who suggested the use of prison labour, accompanied the party, and Mr Robert Coneys, head warder, with six or seven assistants, had the unenviable task of controlling an unruly and unsavoury bunch of criminals. Doctor Porter, Mr Dundas (engineer) and a few others completed the company.

They carried with them all the building material they needed to build barracks and with stores and tools had the means to make this a self-contained efficient unit. A horse and dray was their only transport at the camp which was set up just beyond the tongue of land now known as Sandfly Point. There was a good landing just below the rapids and the buildings were put up just clear of high tide and flood level. Of late years some traces of the old camp have been obliterated but others still remain. The prisoners lived in corrugated iron huts with fifteen to each one. These buildings, with a boatshed, storeroom, cookshop and staff quarters made a compact settlement on the limited area available for building.

The camp was set up on 11 December 1890, and on the thirtieth of the same month two prisoners, Lewis and Williams, made their escape after helping themselves to unguarded stores. They were missed almost immediately, but there weren't enough wardens to spare any to chase after them. It was thought too, that they might come back when they found what they were up against when they reached Lake Ada. They managed, however, to overcome that obstacle, then followed the Track right through to Lake Te Anau. Fortune so far favoured them for they caught the steamer there and were no doubt beginning to congratulate themselves on making a good clean getaway. But they were in for a shock, when they found Inspector Maddern waiting for them when they landed at Te Anau.

Work on the road proceeded leisurely. Apart from a lack of discipline, rainy days were almost as many as work days. It was soon obvious that the scheme was a failure. Some of the more difficult and defiant individuals were taken away and replaced by others, but there was no improvement.

The winter months, when the sun is not seen for several weeks, must have been depressing in the extreme for both prisoners and staff. Before a year had passed one of the prisoners, Michael French, sickened and died. It was whispered that one of his fellow prisoners had contributed to his death by inflicting some injury. He had been in a fight with one, Harry Jackson, when he had received a black eye. This fight witnessed by an assistant warder, Egbert White, took place, he said, on the island. This island would be the spit on which the present Sandfly buildings now stand. It would originally have been an island when the tide was in. A causeway has been built to raise the neck above the highest tides, but a big flood occasionally spills over.

French worked for only an hour and a half on the morning following the fight and from that time his condition worsened until he died on 6 November 1891. At an inquest held the following day the cause of death was declared "disease of the kidneys".

A burial place was selected at the opposite side of the river, some fifty yards from the bank and a picket fence placed round the grave. This fence was still standing in the twenties but by the thirties it had gone and nothing was left to mark the spot.

When searching for it I came across a piece of 4 x 1 sawn timber, pointed and driven into the ground. It had rotted off just above the surface of the ground but was sound underneath. I welcomed this as a possible clue. A few stones were on the surface, the only ones nearby, and in other respects it near-enough corresponded to the place described to me by some men who had visited it many years before. Upon digging, however, I could find no place where the ground had been disturbed. I haven't yet given up hope of finding it, but this hope grows more dim with each unsuccessful search.

A year had nearly passed when another pair of rascals made their escape. This pair, Middleton and M'Guire, got as far as Mossburn, when on Christmas Day they were caught. Middleton gave as his reason for trying to escape, the treatment received at Prison Camp. He said that the food was unfit for men to live on for any length of time. The potatoes were mostly rotten, and some of the meat, especially the salt beef, was bad through being left in the casks in the sun. The flour was also bad, from which the baker could not make good bread. There was a lack of medical supplies and one man lay ten days, part of the time unconscious, before he died. No effort was made to give him medicine or nourishment. The only nourishment he got was a little cocoa to moisten his lips. One day he went to see the sick man. He was then so weak he had not the strength to lift his hand to brush the sandflies from his face and they were free to suck the blood out of him. When he saw men receive such treatment, which he himself might eventually receive, he made up his mind to escape. These apparently were not regarded as sufficient reasons for breaking away and he was awarded an additional two years to his current term and his companion, M'Guire, one.

A year passed with less than a mile of road to show from the effort and it was realised the job would never be accomplished by prison labour. A visit by the Prime Minister, the Hon. R. J. Seddon, showed him the situation and its problems and he now decided that the prisoners were to be removed. He also recommended that a pack track, six feet wide, should be formed instead of the roadway and that the work be done by contract. The decision to break up the Prison Camp was made in April 1892, but it was not till September that the SS *Hinemoa* picked up prisoners and staff and conveyed them to Wellington.

In August, Quintin MacKinnon, returning from a visit to Milford, had brought the rather alarming word that the camp was on the verge of starvation. They had been on short rations for two or three weeks and could not hold out much longer as Donald Sutherland's supplies had been fully drawn upon. On his way back over the Pass, MacKinnon encountered deep snow which had not frozen. He made the trip at considerable risk and had a number of cuts and bruises to show as evidence of his exploit. The Government was notified of the lack of stores and immediately sent some in.

The experiment with prison labour launched so hopefully ended as a failure. Condemned for another winter after a decision made to quit, the frustration and downright misery of the sunless, damp, frozen, half-starved camp, in an atmosphere of ill will bordering on open hostility, tell a tale of woe surpassing anything in the history of the Track.

And yet Sandfly is a beautiful place. In certain lights and atmospheric conditions its charm baffles description. They must have seen sunrises such as one I saw once with the sun over Mt Underwood. There was a very clear atmosphere with a silvery edge to all the objects lighted up. As if it had expended all its polish in illuminating everything it touched and drained itself of brightness, the sun was absorbed by the river and looked up from its depths as a plain silvery disc without an accompanying ray to strike the eye. The tide was well in and the patch of toe toes between the island and the mainland, not partially hidden as they are now with the growing mikimikis, were in duplicate, their heads a silvery plume of extreme delicacy above and below the waterline.

Sights such as this no doubt came to raise the spirits in the cheerless camp. Joy and sorrow, strength and weakness, beauty and plainness have mercifully ever been interwoven. The Maoris were well aware of this for they tell that Tu after his tremendous exertions hacking out this inlet, Poi Poi Tane (Milford Sound) rested on the "Seat of Tu", what we call the Devil's Armchair. While he was reclining there, Te Hine-nui-te-po (the Great Lady of Death) came along to see how the job was progressing, and so beautiful did she find his handiwork she was afraid that when men saw it they would want to live there forever. To remind them of their frailty and mortality she liberated a large namu (sandfly) at Te-namu-a-Te-Hine-nui-te-po (Sandfly Point). This was followed by the addition of other sandflies of ordinary size as well as fleas and mosquitoes. The fleas and mosquitoes don't seem to have thrived but the sandflies see that all the gaps in their ranks are filled.

Quintin MacKinnon, making preparations for the coming season, set sail up the lake on the last day of November 1892, on his way to Milford to make arrangements with Donald Sutherland about meeting track-walkers at Lake Ada. He left Te Anau about midnight, reaching Te Anau Downs at 9.30 in the morning. After getting some supplies he sailed away and was last seen rounding Welcome Point, near the mouth of the Eglinton River. He expected to reach Milford in two days' time and return straightaway.

At first no one worried when he failed to return at the expected time, but after two or three weeks' absence, his friends became anxious for his safety.

On 26 December a party consisting of Captain Meville Duncan, William Snodgrass, Samuel Stevens and an Australian visitor, Dr M'Inerney, set sail in Mr Snodgrass's yacht to find out if they could what had become of MacKinnon. They first made for Garden Point at the entrance of the South Fiord where MacKinnon had his hut. Adverse winds, with hail and sleet, made progress so slow that it was 8 o'clock before they reached it. There was no sign of the hut being occupied for a considerable time. His dog was there and looking quite sleek and well fed, but this was accounted for by the feathers of the kakapo lying round the hut.

Still encountering adverse winds, they started off the next day, taking the dog with them. Reaching Shelter Bay, they spent a rainy night camped on the shingle beach and on the next day arrived at the head of the lake. After examining the places where his boat may have been left, they entered the Government Hut but that had evidently not been used for a long time.

There was still a chance that he may have taken his boat farther up the river so, leaving Captain Duncan with the yacht, the other three set off prepared, if necessary, to go on to Milford. At MacKinnon's hut up the Clinton, two miles from the lake, a brief search showed that their last slender hope of finding trace of him alive had vanished. But they felt it their duty to go on to Milford even if it would only confirm their belief that he had never reached that far.

Next morning they set off for Beech Huts, where they spent that night. The huts showed no signs of being lived in but someone had been there. Going on the next day (New Year's Day) to Milford, they met some men at work on the Track. It was one of them who had visited the Beech Huts. These men had been working on the Track for six weeks and nobody had passed during that time. On arrival at Sutherland's they were told that MacKinnon had not been there for months. At this news they sadly made their way back and rejoined Captain Duncan. In their absence he had rowed all round the head of the lake in a flattie but had seen no sign of oars or wreckage.

Contrary winds again plagued them and they had to make use of the oars to get away and make headway down the lake. They kept a lookout for signs of a boat but as night came on they had to give up and go on to Te Anau Downs.

On their return to Te Anau the next day they reported to the police that MacKinnon was missing, and a preliminary search had found nothing. The Government now took action and sent a search party, equipped for a lengthy period if such was necessary. Thomas McKenzie was asked by the Prime Minister, the Right Hon. Mr Seddon, to take charge of the party which contained six members of the Permanent Artillery, Mr Pillans, McKenzie's exploring companion who volunteered to accompany them, and Captain Brodrick and Constable Green from Te Anau.

Starting off in the steamer (probably the *Te Uira*) they first called at Garden Point then went up the lake to the Middle Fiord at the entrance of which they found Richard Henry who had put in five days searching the western side of the lake. After a cruise round the islands in the arm they steamed across the lake to the Downs. Here they spent the night and the next morning prepared to make a thorough search of the lake shore above Welcome Point.

The steamer was left at the Downs and with the *Gladys*, the small boat they had taken in tow from Te Anau, Henry's *Putangi*, and the *Genesta* (acquired at the Downs) the party deployed, each with a special area to search.

Mr Pillans, Constable Green and Gunners Lawrence and Willis put off in the *Gladys*, three to search the shore and one to coast along in the boat. Messrs Henry and Chamberlain (the latter having joined the party at the Downs) cruised along, taking in the small islands. McKenzie, with Captain Brodrick, Gunners Dale,

Spooner and Corporal Webb went on in the *Genesta* to Catherine Bay, beyond Lone Island, there to establish headquarters, where it was arranged all would rendezvous at 12.30. Corporal Webb and Gunner Spooner were sent northward along the lakeside, Dale was left in charge of the boat, while McKenzie and Captain Brodrick made their way towards Pillans' party.

At eleven o'clock the *Putangi* was seen approaching Lone Island and presently Henry hailed McKenzie with the news that Mac-Kinnon's boat had been found. It lay on its side sunk in six feet of water about a chain distant from Lone Island, between it and the side of the lake. When all hands had arrived it was raised, taken inshore and baled out. The boat evidently had not capsized for all MacKinnon's belongings were in it. But of its owner nothing was to be seen nor anything to indicate the manner of his departure from it. As he had travelled all through the night it is possible he had been overcome with sleep and the boat, suddenly heeling, had thrown him into the water. If he had been wearing his gumboots he would have had difficulty in keeping afloat and regaining the boat. It was said that it was his habit to sit on the high deck at the stern of the boat, as the tiller was very short, and from that position he could easily be dislodged.

The boat would drift inshore until it grounded. When the lake level fell it would heel over, the ballast and what it contained would shift and allow the water to lap in and fill it. When the lake rose again it would remain on the bottom. The boat was twenty-six feet in length and carried five hundredweight of ballast.

On a rocky islet some three chains distant from the sunken boat there stood a huge white granite rock deposited by a glacier in ages gone by. Appealing to the party as an appropriate monumental stone, it was left to Mr Henry to chisel on it at a later date the name of the lost explorer. They now erected a cross near this block, supported it with a cairn of stones, and upon it hung a wreath of myrtle. In this fitting manner they honoured their departed comrade and one whom the country mourned and whose name it would cherish.

After examining the coastline farther on and recovering the boat-fittings found ashore, they returned to the Downs, arriving there at 11.30 pm. Leaving the *Genesta* with its owner, Mr Mellands, of the Te Anau Downs Station, they left for Te Anau in the morning, taking MacKinnon's boat, the *Juliet*, with them.

Thomas McKenzie was called upon to pay a further tribute when he was engaged by the Gaelic Society to select a suitable spot on the Pass for a memorial cairn to be erected to the memory of its discoverer. The place selected, a little mound near the lowest part of the saddle, is probably near the place where he first looked over into the Arthur Valley. This cairn, surmounted with a cross, impressive in its dignified simplicity, calls upon the traveller to consider what he owes to the pathfinder who, with patience and endurance, blazed the trail the tramper now follows.

These tokens, however fittingly they serve, are not the greatest or most enduring monuments to his name. In the four brief years remaining to him after his discovery of the Pass, he gained the reputation of an unparalleled guide, companion, philosopher and trusty friend. The guide at that time had also to be pack horse, cook, doctor, master of bushcraft, carpenter, boatman—a jack of all trades. He was all these and more. His pompolonas or pancakes which gave the name to his camp in the Clinton, were delicacies which proved his skill as a chef. His rich bass voice raised in stirring Gaelic songs when the going began to get tough, put new life into the faltering tramper and encouraged him to keep going. His kindliness and helpfulness endeared him to all whom he met. The records left behind by many people who were privileged to enjoy his expert guidance are monuments that will outlive even those raised in stone.

6

THE TRACK IS FORMED

WITH THE FIASCO of the prison labour project, it seemed as if track plans had been dealt a death blow. The breakdown of the original idea must have quashed enthusiasm for further development. Both effort and money had been squandered on an unprofitable experiment.

Had the services of the surveyors been retained, it is very likely that a road instead of a track would serve the visitors today. As it was, the six-foot-wide track decided upon needed only another foot to make it a serviceable one-lane road.

The new project was now entrusted to the Public Works which started about mid-November, 1892. Early in the season they added two further buildings to the one the surveyors built at Doughboy. One was a storeroom, the other a cookhouse and dining-room. They continued through the season till early in June, when the *Hinemoa* called and carried all hands away for the winter.

In 1893 some thirty men under Edwin Price carried on the work round the lake and beyond. Some of them were recruited from Kumera goldfields. Competent in the use of explosives and familiar with the type of work they met here, they made good progress. On the rock wall, on the side of the track near the top of the bluff walk at the head of Lake Ada, you can see the names of two of these men, "A. Stenhouse, F. W. Mahon, Kumera, May 1898". The work begun in 1892 on the shore of Lake Ada was not completed till 1898. Only a few men would find room to work on the bluff and it was probably the last link on the Sandfly-Beech Huts track to be completed.

Like the surveyors before them they had to carry all their stores and equipment on their backs. Harry Gilmore Smith records that between Sandfly and Doughboy this meant carrying at least fifty pounds each load and making five or more trips a day. To do this each man would travel twenty miles in the course of the day and shift between 250 and 300 pounds a packhorse load. They were paid one shilling and threepence an hour and were quite happy to work for ten hours or more a day.

During the season two large parties from the Sound made a trip to the Sutherland Falls and occasional parties came overland down the valley to Milford.

The 1893-94 season followed with much the same fortune as the previous one, but there was still a lot of track to be formed.

In October 1894 a much larger party was sent to the Sound to speed up the job. There was some criticism of so much money being spent in the Arthur Valley, when most of the tourists merely visited the Sutherland Falls via the Clinton. But it was easier then to supply a work force in the Arthur Valley by sea than one in the Clinton via Te Anau. It was also expected that the shipping companies would bring more excursionists when the track was formed right up to the Sutherland Falls.

Although they lost their champion when Quintin died, the people of Te Anau had not lost their faith in the future of the track. They were fortunate in the men succeeding him and every year saw an improvement in transit by road, lake and track. The steamers were gingered up in their performance by the installation of new boilers, the end of the gravelled road crept nearer to the lake and, sooner or later, they were sure that a well-formed track would cover every mile between Lake Te Anau and Milford Sound.

Shortly after MacKinnon's demise we hear of Richard Henry guiding a steamship excursion party from the Sound to the Sutherland Falls. Late in 1892 we hear of Jack Ross in the capacity of guide. Samuel Stephen, or Steven, also comes into the picture at that time as guide and as the builder of the Mintaro Hut, a year later.

There were others besides these we have named engaged at intervals before Donald Ross was appointed Government Guide, and before he and his brother contracted to maintain the track during the nineties and early years of the new century. The Ross brothers were cousins of Thomas McKenzie, MHR, whose interest in this region doubtless influenced them in their choice of occupation. Donald Ross made regular trips between Te Anau and Milford carrying mail and with a companion, Jack Smith, for a time carried supplies to the work camps.

61

During the 1894-95 season a camp was set up where the surveyors had theirs (Slip Camp), about midway between Boatshed and Quintin. We don't hear of them attempting to supply that camp by the river as the surveyors had done. By this time the track would be formed for most of the way towards Slip Camp and packing would be a better proposition than river transport. Mr Butler was now in charge of the work.

In January 1895 a shadow of gloom was cast over the camp when one of the most popular men of the company sickened, was taken down to Milford, died there and was buried at Cemetery Point. Donald Sutherland brought the sad tidings to the camp. A brief discussion over what was to be done resulted in two of the men being sent over to Lake Te Anau to see if they could catch up with Donald Ross who, two days before, had gone on down there.

It was between four and five o'clock in the afternoon when they set out and neither of them had been over the Pass before. They took a packet of candles and clear, bottomless bottles to serve as lanterns. It was dusk when they reached the Pass and all there was to guide them were poles at intervals. Some were standing, others lying down and, to make sure they did not lose their way, one man would remain at a pole until the other found the next one. In this way they slowly found their way down to the bush in safety. They spent the night at Mintaro and at daybreak the next morning they set off with all speed for the head of the lake. They found Donald just ready to embark at the mouth of the Clinton. Delivering their message they repaired to the hut nearby and enjoyed a well-earned meal and a sleep. They took their time returning to camp.

Work went on without further incident to the end of the season. They were now approaching the Beech Huts but it was not until 1897 that the track, following the right bank of Roaring Creek, passed the place where the present suspension bridge spans the creek at Quintin.

MacKinnon's Track did not cross Moraine and Roaring creeks but kept to their left banks all the way down from a little below the bushline at the foot of the Pass. The new route was selected because it was expected to afford a better grade. It must be remembered that at that time, and for many years later, trampers had to retrace their steps over the track and with their heavy packs the climb up to the Pass over MacKinnon's Track was something of a trial. Had the traffic been all the one way as now, it is unlikely that an alternative route would have been sought.

But it is doubtful if much was gained even at that early time. Three-quarters of a mile was added to the length of the track, the natural grade from Quintin up to Dudleigh Falls on Roaring Creek is as steep as the first half-mile on the other side, while from Moraine Creek to the Pass, another steep section, there is plenty of room to break down the grade into serviceable zigzags. The creeks over the years have been a constant source of trouble. Roaring Creek has claimed two victims, a man (Australian), and a horse.

In 1897 the Union Steamship Company erected two huts for the use of their excursionist passengers when they visited the Sutherland Falls. They were the first buildings on the site the Quintin Huts now occupy, and were a part of the Quintin establishment later on after the abandonment of Beech Huts. They shared the name of Beech Huts with the old ones, until the name Quintin was applied when the Tourist Department took over control early in the new century.

The day-to-day life on the track was recorded in their diaries by the two Ross brothers. Of these priceless records only Jack's from January 1898 to 27 November 1900 has survived. This tells of the rugged life at that time before the introduction of pack-horses, the constant combat with flood rains and the endless repetition of guiding over the familiar miles, including at times the lakes and the Sound.

Late in the season in 1898 Jack Ross put up a log bridge at Quintin linking it with the new track. The track from Milford to the falls was now in first-class condition and was being pushed on up to the Pass.

Each season's work made the track easier to pass over and the numbers of trampers steadily increased. Eventually the Clinton Valley received attention. A primitive hut between Lake Mintaro and the Pass was put up in 1889, but it was not much used and its life short. Tents at the present site did service until the first hut was built in 1894. In the same year one was put up at Mid Camp (Six Mile). From early times Quintin MacKinnon had a camp at Pompolona, but the first serviceable hut in the valley was his Two Mile Hut. This hut, two miles from the mouth of the river, was at the navigable limit for his whaleboat. The Government Hut at the mouth of the river was put up in 1890, and the track from it led behind a swampy area a half-mile up from the mouth of the river, to cut across a wide bend and regain the river a little above MacKinnon's hut. In 1895 Angus W. McBean built the first Glade House for J. F. Garvey and it was opened early in 1896. Glade House guests walking the track were ferried across the river and followed it up past MacKinnon's hut. This same route is followed today, except that they now cross the river on a suspension bridge.

Between the tramping seasons, the Ross brothers cut wood across the lake from Te Anau for the steamer. They explored the arms of the lake, always on the lookout for a profitable outcrop of coal, but found only a poor quality lignite. Once while they were visiting Middle Arm, their dog caught a takahe. It was still alive when they got it but was not far from dead. They hurried down to Te Anau to get it away while it was still fresh. This bird may now be seen in the Dunedin Museum. As years went by without others being sighted, it was considered they were extinct. There is no doubt some had been seen, but not identified, before Dr Orbell found a colony of them in Takahe Valley between Lake Te Anau and the coast. Donald and Jack Ross did not share the popular belief they were extinct as they had later heard their call.

In the late nineties, about the end of the year of 1897 or early 1898, occurred an event of prime importance to Milford Track patrons. This was the arrival at Te Anau of the *Tawera*, a seventy-foot steamship for passenger traffic on the lake. Its launching in 1899 marked the end of the period of pioneer and primitive lake transport and inaugurated a service which to the present day happily welcomes and introduces to the Milford Track the thousands of trampers who each season come to enjoy it.

The lake, which in the beginning was a hazard for small craft and more of a hindrance than help to exploration, was now a welcome additional feature to enjoy. Like others in mountainous regions, it can suddenly change from a peaceful calm to a mood of savage intensity, taking unawares both the wary and the unwary. Especially down the arms, the winds may come hurtling and whip up the surface of the lake into a fury. There have been many tales of narrow escapes, but surprisingly few victims. The various vessels propelled by sail and oar sometimes took days traversing its length, and voyagers had to spend the nights ashore; but this did not deter the early visitor. The *Ripple* and *Te Uira,* still wary of the

e lower landing, three-quarters of
mile below Boatshed on the Arthur
ver. Here the trampers were ferried
oss the river from 1901, when the
dge spanning the river above Boat-
ned was washed away, until 1957.

Teddy, a local character, at Sandfly Point.

RIGHT: Mitre Peak from the
wharf at Milford Sound.

BELOW: Lady of the Snows
(*centre*) reflected in Lake Stephen.

ABOVE: The author taking observations in the jungle between Lake Brown and Joe's River.

RIGHT: The plaque of the memorial cairn at Mac-Kinnon Pass.

The MacKinnon Pass Hut in 1970.

A track party at Quintin in 1970.

weather, and taking ten or twelve hours to reach the head of the lake, invited only praise for the service they gave.

The hull of the *Tawera* was built in Dunedin and railed to Mossburn in two sections. From there it was carted by two bullock teams to Te Anau. The boiler, weighing between six and seven tons, was hauled by a horse team driven by Jack Gibson. William Harrison contracted to cart the whole ship and accessories for £150. The waggon for the boiler was built by Burrows of Dipton for £10. The wheels and axle for it were taken from Harrison's mill and put back after the job had been done.

William Harrison and J. O'Callaghan drove the first bullock team of sixteen which were just being broken in. Jack Ryan and Nat Cunningham drove the other team of eight, two of which lost their footing in crossing the Mararoa, and after being dragged out were left for dead. The record doesn't say if mouth-to-mouth resuscitation was resorted to before they were abandoned but, coming round and having no load to hamper them, they caught up with the column a few miles farther on.

After delivering the *Tawera* the bullock teams backloaded wool from Manapouri to Mossburn. The owners of the *Tawera* were the Ross brothers, Donald and John, and Captain R. Murray-Menzies. The cost when it was launched on the lake about February 1899 was £2,200.

In 1901 the Department of Tourist and Health Resorts was established. The transfer of natural assets, hitherto under the control of the Lands Department, took place on 31 July 1901, when all papers and documents were transferred to the Tourist Department. The department, however, did not assume direct administrative control of the Milford Track until 1 October 1903. Prior to this the Track was maintained by contractors, who also retained guiding fees.

John Ross married in 1898 and made Te Anau his headquarters. No doubt he found, as others engaged on the Track have done, that this is not an ideal set-up for married life. So, when the Tourist Department decided it would not renew the maintenance contract, he and Donald probably considered this as good a time as any to make a change.

The departure of the Ross brothers was much deplored. They had seen the Track advance through its developmental stages until there was a well-formed track right through from Lake Te Anau

E

to Milford Sound. They had seen the numbers of tourists treble and had upheld the standard of guiding in the best MacKinnon tradition.

A newspaper correspondent at that time commented that guides of the calibre of the Ross brothers were born, not made, and they would be hard to replace.

With the completion of the track formation, good sound huts at intervals along the Track, a chair over the Arthur River, first-class steamer on the lake, an oil launch *Lizzie* put into service at the Sound by Donald Sutherland and the purchase by the department of Glade House, all seemed set for a prosperous future. The department was fortunate in its choice of Track Manager, Robert Murrell, who with his staff, attended to the maintenance of the entire Track and guided those who required their services.

In this manner ended a period of interesting development which was destined to pave the way for a fuller use and appreciation of this already famous walk.

7

THE TOURIST DEPARTMENT ENTERS

THE ASSUMPTION OF DIRECT CONTROL and supervision of the Milford Track by the Tourist Department resulted in a greater appreciation by the Government of its needs in maintenance and in service to track patrons.

The provisioning and staffing of the huts, long advocated by successive guides and others interested in the track, was now put into operation. The excellent service given by the Garvey family set a standard the Tourist Department could well emulate, but first the huts had to be upgraded to house the staff and provide the necessary facilities for cooking and serving.

Glade House was bought from Mr Garvey in 1903 and extended. Additional huts were in use at Quintin, but the former Beech Huts had had their day. In 1904 a dining-room, storeroom and kitchen were erected and additions were made to the dormitories. The timber for these buildings was pitsawn near the site. The sawpit may still be seen near the horse track, a few chains from the buildings.

In 1906 Garvey's original building was replaced by a new hostel, and Pompolona was chosen as a more suitable site for a lodge than Mintaro and building was started there. Packhorses were introduced and they lifted the burden from the shoulders of the doughty guides.

The Tourist Department bought the Te Anau Hotel and also the lake steamer *Tawera*. Until then it was optional whether track walkers engaged individual guides or whether they went through under their own steam. With the abolition of the guiding fees all were placed on the same footing under the supervision of the guides.

At the other end of the Track Donald Sutherland was not idle. He had already acquired his oil launch, the *Lizzie*, and now telephone connection was made between Sandfly Point and Milford. A party would not have long to wait before the launch, in answer to a call, would be seen turning into the river and heading for the Point. He could now take a full party, unlike earlier, when for want of accommodation some would be left to wait for the return of the lucky ones. Donald, they say, took unholy pleasure in making his selection to fill his boat. Without the trappings, but with the insolent assurance of the bone-pointing witch-doctor, his pointing finger would accompany the verdict of "You and you and you", irrespective of family and other connections. The tariff at Sutherland's Chalet was 10/- per day and the cruise down the Sound in the *Lizzie* was the same figure.

During the 1907-08 season a visitor to the Track whom we may place alongside Donald Sutherland and Quintin MacKinnon in making it known was Miss Blanche E. Baughan. Her description of the scenery and her experience on the Track submitted to the English journal, the *Spectator*, so impressed the editor that in publishing it he changed her heading, "A Notable Walk", to "The Finest Walk in the World". This gift from the gods was naturally seized upon by the Tourist Department to make known to the world its commanding scenic attractions. On her two later visits Miss Baughan declared she was "amazed afresh by this notable walk".

Compared with its condition in the nineties the Track was now something of a cake-walk. A visitor who in 1909 made his ninth trip over it during a period of sixteen years wrote: "Compared with early days the present accommodation is simply luxurious. There were no bridges, very little track and that only blazed, no food, no blankets, no hutkeepers and only the roughest kind of shelter. We had to carry tent, food, clothes and bedding. When we got to a hut, often wet through and always tired, we had to chop wood, make a fire, cook and generally do for ourselves. What would some of our friends say to the walk then?"

The Track must have been in good order to have allowed Andrew McKenzie, Sutherland's stepson, to carry the crankshaft of the *Lizzie*, 100 pounds in weight, over it in eleven hours, a feat that would take some beating.

In 1909, a footbridge was built over the Arthur River about a quarter-mile above Boatshed. This replaced the chair that had been the earlier means of crossing. Unfortunately its life span was short, serving about only two seasons when a high flood carried it away, as another had taken the chair. After that time no attempt was made to restore a fixed crossing and trampers had to go a mile down the river where they were ferried across it. Two very interesting and attractive features, the Mackay Falls and Bell Rock, were now off the visiting list, and were not restored for many decades.

The Track reopened late in 1918, after the end of World War I. Much work had to be done to restore the Track and put the huts in order.

In 1919 the Milford pioneer Donald Sutherland died. He had been ill for some time, and had fallen from his bed. He was so heavy a man that Mrs Sutherland could not lift him back into it. There he remained until two months later when the first vessel called, and Sutherland was given burial in a spot near his cottage. Mrs Sutherland was urged to accompany the visitors and return to friends and relatives, but she preferred to stay on in isolation. Nor did she again leave, apart from a brief visit to Dunedin, during the next five years, after which she too joined her husband in the grave now graced by well-kept surrounds.

There was some dislocation in the accommodation of trampers at Milford in the first years of the post-war period. Sutherland's Chalet was no longer available for full parties and the buildings at Sandfly Point were far from adequate to accommodate the numbers going through.

During the 1919-20 season tragedy struck in the loss of a Dunedin lady, Miss Reid, who, without the guide's permission or knowledge, had gone ahead while snow lay on the Pass and was never seen again. A party returning over the Pass met her as she arrived at the top of the Pass and that was the last seen of her. At first it was thought that she fell over the cliff into the Roaring Creek Valley but a search made there by a most competent climber, Sam Turner, found nothing. Turner also made an underwater search of the tarns on the Pass.

A few years ago a lady going through the Track said that her father, who was in the party from which Miss Reid disappeared, thought that the most likely place she would wander off would be just after crossing Moraine Creek, the first large creek on the way down from the Pass. This is an area exposed to avalanches from Jervois Glacier and when they happen the Track is obliterated for about 100 yards. The tendency then is to follow down the creek instead of looking for the track leading from it. When the Track, after an avalanche, has not been well-marked I have seen some trampers temporarily wander from it. The terrain farther down the creek is extremely rough with boulders great and small covered by fern and stunted bush. One could fall down a crevice between the rocks and if injured find difficulty in getting out.

When the party following the one from which Miss Reid was lost reached Milford they found Mrs Sutherland looking up and down the opposite bank of the Cleddau. She said she had heard the sound of a whistle. It was not known at the time but discovered later, that Miss Reid had actually carried a whistle, and a puzzling doubt remains whether she may have reached that distance and perhaps drowned in attempting to cross the river which then ran close by the Milford Lodge. These and many other theories have been mooted to account for her disappearance but no one really knows what happened.

During the 1920-21 season additional accommodation became available at Pompolona and Quintin. At Sandfly Point two new huts were put up, and Mr and Mrs Adams were appointed host and hostess. The telephone line was restored right through from Glade House to Milford. That same year the *Tawera* was converted from a steamer to a motor vessel and a new launch was bought for Milford Sound.

The following season, 1921-22, was numerically a particularly poor one, with less than 300 arriving at Glade House. Probably the financial depression of that time was mainly responsible for this decline in numbers.

The Tourist Department report for the 1923-24 season records that 420 people arrived at Glade House, most of them making the journey in five and a quarter days to, from and including the stay at Milford. It claims that this reflects the excellent condition of the Track at that time.

In the beginning of the 1924-25 season Mr L. M. Cheriton was appointed manager of the Milford Track following Mr P. E. Challis, who for many years had held that position. Owing to the late arrival of the government steamer *Tutanekai*, stores for Quintin and Sandfly Point had to be packed from Glade House, a tedious task that not only hindered track work but the frequent passage of horses over the Pass ruined much of the lately repaired track there. Nevertheless much good work was accomplished during the season. Five bridges were built between Glade and Pompolona

and one over Camp Oven Creek, a mile from Sandfly. Sutherland's Chalet was demolished and some of the timber used to put
up a boatshed at Sandfly Point. A new wharf was erected at the
head of Lake Te Anau, replacing the one wrecked by floodwaters
from the Glade Burn which had changed its course.

With depressing regularity track history records the brief times
when all seemed set for a trouble-free, prosperous period, only to
have those hopes washed away in disastrous floods, buried in slips
and avalanches, or turned to ashes by fire. The year 1924 saw the
wharf at the head of Lake Te Anau wrecked; in 1925 Pompolona
was wrecked by the blast from an avalanche; and in 1926 Sandfly
was destroyed by fire. Glade House was destroyed by fire in 1928,
but rebuilt shortly afterwards.

The Sandfly fire was particularly disastrous because the hotel
at Milford, which would make Sandfly obsolete, was shortly
to be constructed. Because of this, there was little enthusiasm in rebuilding at Sandfly. But, with the minimum of
reasonable accommodation, supplemented by tents, the gap was
bridged between the fire and the opening of the new hotel in
December 1928.

In the same year a hut was placed on the MacKinnon Pass.
It was put up by Ivan Latham, who, as Ministry of Works
carpenter, was a familiar figure on the Track and at Milford for
some thirty years.

The hut was prefabricated and packed by horses to the Pass.
The arched iron roof made packing next to impossible and the
packer, losing patience with it, set on to it with his axe and
whacked each arched section into two. The hut was small, but
parties at that time would normally reach no more than twenty,
and by the time the last tramper put in an appearance the first
would be gone. To be able to enjoy their lunches in this haven
with the luxury of a cup of tea was indeed a welcome addition to
the comforts the Track provided.

With the Milford Hotel opened and the Pass Hut in service the
trampers were now well catered for but ill fortune still dogged their
steps. On New Year's Day Glade House was burned to the
ground. A party of four men who left Glade House that morning
to go over Dore Pass looked down and saw it go up in flames.
Among those of a newly-arrived party viewing the conflagration at
closer quarters was a lady who was later to meet one of the Dore

Pass party and marry him, which indicates that romance can bud and thrive even amid scenes of disaster.

The economic depression of the early thirties affected the Track with the numbers of walkers falling off considerably. In 1932 very good work was done at Quintin in building an ablution block, drying rooms, and installing an electric lighting system. The materials were hauled by tractor and sledge over the Track. The tractor was a Cletrac, narrow-gauge machine, which expeditiously landed, besides all the other stores, heavy units which could not be packed by horses. At the same time, material for a suspension bridge to span Roaring Creek was brought to replace the old original log and slab bridge built by Jack Ross.

Steel was brought in for bridges at Camp Oven Creek between Sandfly and Doughboy; at a creek midway between Boatshed and Quintin; another, one and a half miles from Quintin, and a fourth at the top of Gentle Annie, three-quarters of a mile from Quintin. Today's walkers have a constant reminder of those days in the hardened remains of bags of cement which had got wet and were jettisoned at the foot of Gentle Annie and the wrecked steel bridges, one near the top of Gentle Annie and the other on the far side of the river about three miles from Quintin.

The track beginning at Deep Water Basin leading to Grave-Talbot Pass by way of a suspension bridge over the Cleddau, above the Gulliver River, enabled trampers to make that journey in safety. During the 1932-33 season thirteen trampers, one a lady, crossed the Grave-Talbot Pass.

That was a very wet season, February experiencing nineteen days' continuous rain. No wonder glowing reports were heard of the newly-built drying-rooms and hot showers at Quintin. February, one of the driest months in the year, occasionally outstrips all the other months in rainfall. (The record wet year 1958 recorded sixty-nine inches in February's twenty-nine days.) In contrast, the next season 1933-34 was a very dry one, with no floods until the end of March.

There was now a great change afoot and it was hard to believe that at last there was the likelihood of an open road to Milford via Eglinton and Cleddau valleys becoming a reality. In 1934 the road from Te Anau was pushed through as far as the Divide and plans formed to take the road up the Hollyford Valley and, by a tunnel, right through to Milford Sound.

As W. H. Homer had noted sixty-five years before the Homer Saddle from its height of 4,480 feet drops on one side to the Cleddau Canyon which descends precipitously to Milford Sound.

When this tunnel was finally completed, it entered from the Hollyford end at 3,023 feet above sea level, extended for three-quarters of a mile on a grade of one in ten to a height of 2,600 feet on the Milford side.

For the approach to the tunnel, much of the road to Marion Camp had to be laboriously blasted out of rock by pre-mechanised means. With their picks, shovels and wheelbarrows the tunnellers reached the approach by mid-1935 and went digging underground by early 1936.

It was hazardous work, often in conditions of heavy rain and snow, with the workmen living first in tents and then in the permanent camp huts. As the tunnel entrance is right underneath a snowfield, avalanches happened frequently, and in July 1936 one man, P. L. Overton, was killed and others were injured in an avalanche. Another tragedy occurred in May 1937 with two deaths and three men injured. This time the engineer-in-charge, D. T. Huber, was killed, as was T. W. Smith, the tunnel overseer.

Despite the dangers and difficulties in this project, the Milford side was pierced in March 1940.

After this the work of enlargement of the tunnel continued at a good pace until in early 1942 all work was halted when equipment was transferred to more urgent war projects. But later in that same year an American drove his car through the unfinished tunnel.

It was not until after the war that work was resumed on the tunnel, and although trucks were allowed through earlier, it was not until the 1954-55 season that private cars were allowed through. Up till then buses would leave tourists at one side to walk through, to be picked up by another waiting bus on the other side of the tunnel.

On 1 March 1934 the last survey peg was driven in in front of the Hotel Milford, seventy-three-and-three-quarter miles from Te Anau.

But already in the thirties, with the road opening up the Eglinton Valley, more trampers were encouraged to use the Dore and Grave-Talbot passes. The Dore Pass leads from behind Glade House over the Earl Mountains to the Eglinton Valley. Still, however, the great bulk of the Milford Track walkers returned, as they had come, via the MacKinnon Pass.

The year 1936 was notable for the vice-regal visits, when their Excellencies Lord and Lady Galway and family went up the Track from Milford in November as far as Quintin. Then Lady Galway and party in March made the trip over from Glade House and back.

During the thirties Milford saw increasing activity in shipping circles. In 1936 the *Marama* called on twelve occasions and the *Wanganella* once, also HMS *Wellington* and the American yacht *Idgrasil*. In 1937 the *Marama* called on ten trips to and from Melbourne. Over eighty passengers landed direct from Australia, starting their New Zealand tour from Milford Sound. Others embarked after their tour had ended with a walk over the Milford Track. The *Maunganui* made two direct cruises from Sydney to Milford Sound and one from Wellington. The *Wanganella* also made one visit from Wellington. These cruises were fully booked.

In 1938 the *Maunganui* called on five trips direct from Melbourne, disembarking over 100 visitors who began their tour of New Zealand via the Milford Track. The following year the *Maunganui* made fifteen calls, landing 170 passengers.

Other interesting items may be noted in the Tourist Department Reports. To quote extracts:

1936

> It is now possible to motor to the Homer Hut via the Eglinton Road which will make the Grave-Talbot route more popular. The new launch, *Donald Sutherland*, arrived in February.
>
> Eighty men will continue working on this side (Milford) during the winter, necessitating a regular service from Bluff, the first winter that Milford will have sea communications. In previous years we have been isolated for sixteen weeks.
>
> Mr P. H. Long (Manager Hotel Milford) reports that a new bridge over the Clinton River (at Glade) has been completed and is very satisfactory. Good work has been done here.

1938

> It will be possible next season to motor to the Chasm, a distance of six miles from the hotel.
>
> The Department took over control of the Lake Te Anau launch *Tawera*.
>
> Lake Ada has been very difficult to negotiate this season

owing to the very low water-level. The service has been maintained with difficulty.

Pioneers in air travel to Milford Sound appear in the next two reports:

1939

Mr Bradshaw of Southland made three successful landings in the district during the past year. He landed twice on the sandspit at Lake Ada and once on the beach at Deep Water Basin, about one mile from the hotel.

1940

Captain Mercer (Air Travel NZ) landed on the beach at Deep Water Basin, July 16, 1939. He examined the place in view of regular landing. With comparatively little outlay he considered a landing place could be made.

Entry in Milford Hotel Day Book:

First party to leave hotel through Homer Tunnel, 17/3/40.

Continuing Tourist Department Report:

1941

The Milford Track has been well patronised during the past season, quite a number making the round trip via the tunnel.

1942

Track opened December 20, 1942.

This was merely a flash in the pan, for it closed early in the New Year. War again intervened and now we must await five long years before again hearing the merry voices of the happy wanderers.

While the Track was closed during the years of the Second World War, it seemed that nature was in league with the forces of destruction let loose in the theatres of battle. While Herculean efforts were made to save the world from slipping back into the jungle, the Track, left to its own devices, actually did that very thing.

The winters were exceptionally severe. Tremendous slips and avalanches obliterated miles of the Track. Mighty beech trees with a multitude of their lesser brethren crashed down across it. Steel bridges securely anchored in concrete were torn from their solid beds and brought to rest hundreds of yards from where they stood. Scores of wooden bridges were never seen again. The Arthur River for a distance of a quarter of a mile was forced to find a new bed. Where William Quill and his companions fifty years before brought stores in their boat to Slip Camp, the riverbed built up to make navigation impossible. Alternating with the destruction in winter, rapid growth springing up through the debris in summer made the confusion a tangled jungle.

The manager of the Milford Hotel, Mr Berndtson and his wife, were the first to make the attempt to reach Quintin from Milford on 23 March 1944. Thoroughly familiar with the Track before it was closed and as fit as anyone to tackle it now, they struggled on, over, under and between fallen timber, slashing an opening where they could find no passage, fording streams where the bridges had gone, including the rocky bed of the formidable Poseidon, then at the bluff below Boatshed coming up against what appeared to be an impassable barrier. The narrow ledge, which when clear gave many a tramper some worried moments, was now a repository for many trees, precariously clinging to the ledge on their way down from the heights above. With a twenty-foot drop into the river, scooped out to a depth of perhaps fifty feet at this bend, Mr and Mrs Berndtson grimly edged their way till, after great difficulty and danger, they were able to heave a sigh of relief when they found they were again in comparative safety.

They had left Sandfly Point at 9 am and forded the Arthur River at 5 pm. This stretch is normally walked in two and a half to three hours. They spent the night at Boatshed and the next morning, after making a quarter-mile, slashing their way and crawling under and over masses of fallen timber, they decided it was futile to proceed further. A strong party with more time and more supplies was clearly called for. They returned to Milford after what they described as a most arduous and unpleasant trip.

The next inspection was made by Mr George Auld, accompanied by Mr Berndtson and two others. Mr Auld at that time was in charge of the road construction between the tunnel and Milford.

They went in at Glade on 21 January 1945, carrying enough provisions to last for three or four days. They found the track from Lake Te Anau to the Pass not so bad, but from Quintin to Boatshed they had to slash their way through fallen timber and second growth. The weather deteriorated and with the Arthur River in flood they retraced their steps back to Quintin. With their supplies running low they made an inspection of the pre-war stores and found a tin of biscuits, by no means improved by age, but with some treatment in the oven they were put on the menu along with some cold tinned meat.

76

The next day, with rain still pouring down, they found the river, as before, too high to cross. They stayed the night at Boatshed and the next day, with the river still in the same condition, Mr Berndtson swam across with a line. The packs were taken over the line, then the others swam across. Poseidon Creek presented another hazard. It could not be crossed at the usual ford as the current was far too strong, but farther down where it was held to a mild flow by the swollen lake, they made a crossing though it took them up to their necks.

Wet, tired and hungry, they arrived at Sandfly Point thankful to board Mr Berndtson's dinghy and finish their ordeal. After a reviving hot shower, a change into dry clothes and a good square meal, they were able to enjoy their exploits in retrospect. In luxurious comfort Mr Auld was now able to write up his report. The continuous rain had prevented him from taking down notes in his notebook as he went along but the facts were well impressed on his memory.

The terrible condition of the Track gave rise to fears that its restoration, on economic grounds, might not be justified; but optimism prevailed and preparations were made to put it back in working order.

An early start was made in the 1946-47 season to clear the Track but it was not till late in the season, 1 March, that it was officially opened. In February of that year a vice-regal party went through the Track. The Governor, Sir Bernard Freyberg and Lady Freyberg attended by Michael Cole and Rosemary Eley, and accompanied by Mr Berndtson, made the trip while the Track was still in a rough condition and the huts not all staffed. Sandy Brown, track foreman, was host and chef, rising to the occasion as to the manner born. The party adjusted itself to the rough conditions on the track and enjoyed the novelty of the primitive conditions.

The next season 1947-48, the first full season after the war, was exceptionally wet, but the Track was well patronised even though it was in no way restored to its pre-war condition when it was reopened. It had been well managed and well maintained between the two world wars. The Track was parcelled out between the staff, each trackman having a certain length to keep in order. From huts spaced at convenient distances, they were always near their work. They were right on the spot when a sudden need arose to restore a bridge, clear away a slip or remove a fallen tree. Each man took a pride in his work and tried to have his section compare favourably with his neighbour's. Some of the men had been on the Track many years; Albert Hicky put in thirteen consecutive seasons. Messrs R. Murrell, P. E. Challis and L. M. Cheriton are names which recall long and good service.

Frequent changes in staff, no matter how good the men may be, do not give time to gain the experience necessary to cope with the special problems met with on the Track. Experience teaches one how to deal with trouble not only when it arises, but when and where to anticipate it.

After the war there was sufficient staff to maintain the Track, but not, at the same time, to restore it to its former condition. There were still scores of creeks crying out for bridges and places needing much work to divert water from the Track. Times were changing and men were not so willing as in the past to isolate themselves in the lonely track huts. From the staffed huts there is almost as much time spent walking to and from some of the jobs as working on them. The time has come when the Track should be made to take a vehicle which will deposit men and tools on the job in a matter of minutes instead of hours.

The next two seasons, 1948-49 and 1949-50, were very wet. During the former, 1,200 people went through the Track, a record number to that date. They were difficult seasons for the track staff, guiding the trampers through and trying to maintain the Track.

There was no let-up in the numbers walking the Track in the early part of the 1949-50 season. The couple at Quintin, Mr and Mrs Smith, battling along on their own, threw in the sponge and walked out in February. In fairness to the Tourist Department it may be stated that additional help was available and actually sent, but the couple preferred to work on their own.

When my wife and I replaced them the season was far advanced and the numbers going through had tapered off. The weather too had improved and until the busy period at Easter we were able to hold the fort unaided.

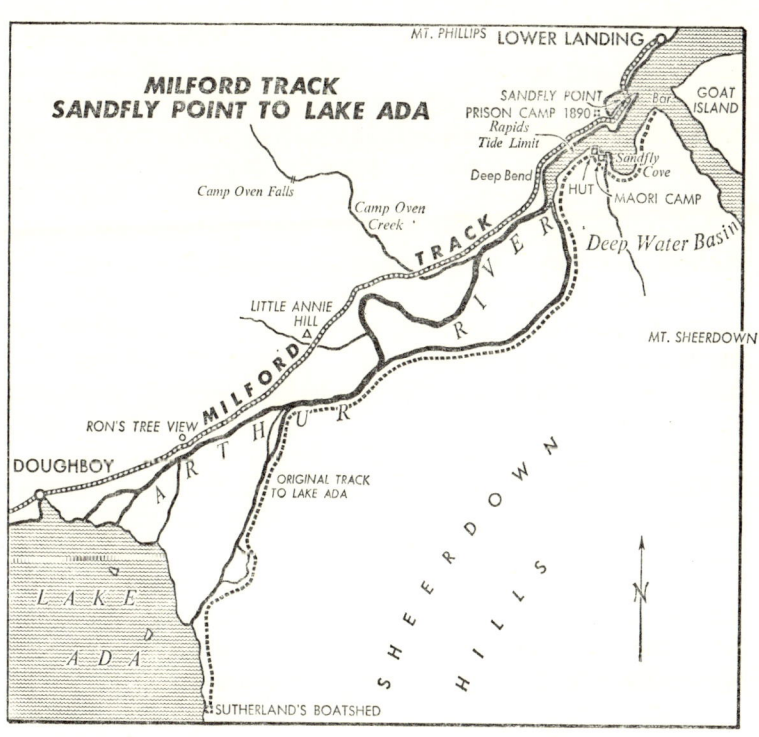

MILFORD TRACK
SANDFLY POINT TO LAKE ADA

MT. PHILLIPS LOWER LANDING

SANDFLY POINT
PRISON CAMP 1890
Rapids
Tide Limit

Deep Bend

Camp Oven Falls

Camp Oven
Creek

TRACK

RIVER

Sandfly
Cove

HUT

MAORI CAMP

Deep Water Basin

GOAT
ISLAND

Bar

LITTLE ANNIE
HILL

MILFORD

ARTHUR

MT. SHEERDOWN

RON'S TREE VIEW

DOUGHBOY

ORIGINAL TRACK
TO LAKE ADA

LAKE

ADA

SHEERDOWN

HILLS

SUTHERLAND'S BOATSHED

N

79

8

WE TAKE OVER AT QUINTIN

AFTER OUR ARRIVAL early in 1950 we soon settled into the routine of running Quintin. An early start in the morning was the key to a successful day with the kitchen fire the first to receive attention. We were well supplied with wood but as it was by no means tinder dry, I would fill the warming oven with small splinters and chips at night and found that by morning this kindling had dried sufficiently to give the fire a good start. Coal, always lagging behind demand, was used sparingly. Like money, one can use a lot of it if one has it but gets along with surprisingly little when obliged to.

On the days when the trampers went on to Milford there was no chance of getting down to work until the last one had gone. Many little attentions were needed by the departing guests and most wished to chat before we said goodbye and wished them good journeying for the remainder of their trip.

The incoming guests likewise appreciated a welcome and they too frequently asked for repairs to footwear and to the feet as well.

At intervals, heavy rain would pin the trampers down at the huts for a day or more. We had just let a party go one morning when Mr Berndtson rang Quintin from Milford. He asked what the weather was like and I told him I had seen it worse.

"I think you had better hold them," he said.

"They've just gone," I replied, "but I can get them back." I raced out, caught up with the one in the rear and got the word passed along to those in the lead. A half-hour later the rain really got down to business and had the party gone on they would have had difficulty in reaching Boatshed, and from there could have gone no farther. Another time during the following season they were held up at Boatshed. Brian Blackie, packman, and Jack Sullivan, boatman, acted as hosts. They surveyed the meagre stores of food while Brian surreptitiously selected something edible from a scruffy lot of potatoes.

On the Anderson Track.

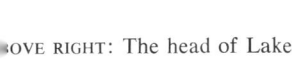

ABOVE: Eighty-seven-year-old
Mr Crothall going strong at
Boatshed.

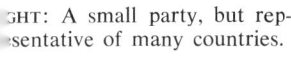

ABOVE RIGHT: The head of Lake
Te Anau.

RIGHT: A small party, but rep-
resentative of many countries.

Embarking at Te Anau.
Skipper Robbie Robb third
from right.

Looking up the Arthur
Valley.

Around the piano at Quintin.

RIGHT: Clinton Valley from the Pass. The Park
Board Huts is in the bush near Lake Mintaro, and
Pompolona in the bush in the distance.

The weather poses many problems even to the most weather-wise. On his way up to Quintin one afternoon with the packhorses, Jock Peterson crossed the first big creek approaching Racecourse Flat, but the rain suddenly became very heavy and put the next creek, a quarter-mile farther on, so high he couldn't attempt it. He returned, but by now the first one was running high. The idea of spending the night in the rain was no more tempting than the turbulent creek so he tried to make a crossing. He managed it all right but he was washed off his feet and only managed to pull himself out on to the right side by snatching at a branch which fortunately was strong enough for Jock to use as a rope.

At that time, as well as the regular parties coming through from Te Anau, the occasional small party would go through from Milford. Te Anau and Milford staff were also at liberty to walk the Track during their off-days. They would arrange with their co-workers for the extra time necessary and repay when the latter in turn made the trip, but we had only an occasional brief hour or two for a jaunt on the Track.

At Quintin the greatest lack, we found, was reading material. The two Southland dailies and the *Otago Daily Times* were supplied but, by the time we got them, were very frequently old news to the incoming guests. We commandeered everything that came our way. I found a few copies of children's comics in an out-of-the-way corner in the storeroom but had misgivings about putting them on the shelf to be read. I thought it might be taken as an insult to their intelligence, but I needn't have worried. They did the worrying, going for them like an aggressive terrier at a stray cat. I appealed to Milford for any reading material they could spare. With commendable promptitude Milford donated a choice selection of books recovered from the Ark. Along with the comics they made a beautifully balanced literary diet, a blending of ancient and modern, the erudite and ridiculous, and our guests thrived on them.

Books are not so much in demand as digests, magazines and lighter reading; trifles one can pick up to browse through and discard. With something to read, a tired person will settle down and relax. Many a tramper, footsore and exhausted on arrival, picks up a magazine before he settles down. With it and his cup of tea, for the time being his aches and pains forgotten, he will find his energy and spirit restored and, minus his pack, want to

81

F

run and skip all the way up to the falls. Reading material and games are like food and drink to the average tramper, in the evenings and on stormbound days, yet this service is often neglected by the management. Tattered magazines are left lying around and in the bunks, and for tidiness sake this great boon is often withheld.

To provide for the lack of games I cut up an old broom-handle into draughtsmen and dyed the blacks with washing blue. Surprisingly, some of these survived until recent times and may possibly still be there.

The old-fashioned fireplaces in the dormitories were huge. I could walk into them with a log on my shoulder. The woodcutters made no objection to collecting the necessary fuel, but supplying the voracious kitchen range was a major job in itself, so I undertook to service the open fires. At that time old stumps, logs and fern covered the clearing close up to the buildings except at the entrance and on a narrow strip on the other side, which was cluttered with clothes lines. To me this situation seemed a chance to manage two jobs at once. I could clear the ground while tapping a handy source of firewood. I gathered the most stodgy and waterlogged wood, of which there was plenty, built that up at the back of the fireplace and, with better wood in front, left it ready for the match. Lighted or unlighted, this stack of wood filled the guests with awe. When the weather was too warm for fires some guests were very eager to see it lighted just to see what would happen. On a cold wet day I would light up just as the first arrivals were expected, so that they would be greeted with a cheery blaze.

I was on my knees applying the match one day when I heard footsteps approach and stop behind me. This was the first arrival. Presently a voice asked, "Is that what I think it is?"

"Yes," I replied, without looking round.

"I thought it was," Miss Footsteps said, "but I've never in all my life seen another like it."

These fires would dry the wet wood as it burned slowly back and sometimes continue burning all night. They were one of Quintin's greatest assets. Of an evening there would be a big semicircle of tired trampers round the fire sitting comfortably in various postures. Sometimes May would say, "Would you like to have your supper right there?" Nothing pleased them better than to be given a pot of tea and a loaf or two of bread with which to make toast for themselves.

The biggest problem was keeping up the supply of linen. Every hour of drying weather had to be grabbed. There was no hot water laid on to the laundry, no washing machine, and the washing copper, to be ready for the sheets, had to be lit at six o'clock in the morning. Making lunches for the departing guests to take with them was another time-consuming job which May tackled cheerfully. We were certainly kept busy, but we found the track staff and guests extremely co-operative and helpful, and enjoyed every day we spent there.

About a week after our settling in at Quintin a hint came down from the track that an old lady was on her way to Quintin. The phone message was vague. Her status as track walker was in doubt as it lacked official blessing and no one was sure whether she might be intending only to make the trip up the lake to Boatshed, then return. What did seem highly probable was that she might expire on her way up to Quintin.

Suddenly it occurred to us, "Would it be that old lady who came in with us on the bus?" Bus passengers at that time had to go through the Homer Tunnel on foot, but nothing daunted, she had stepped out of the bus into the snowstorm and made her way up the hill to the tunnel entrance.

Halfway through the tunnel we in the truck had caught up with her, drenched by the almost ice-cold water which came down from the tunnel roof. We hauled her aboard and, surprisingly, she survived the ordeal.

Years before, on its way back to England, her ship had called at Milford Sound, and thereafter Milford beckoned with such insistence that she determined she would return and, for good measure, include the Track as well. The war intervened, followed by travel restrictions. She was getting no younger, but time only sharpened and tempered her resolution and now, after anticipating this moment for so long and coming so far for its fulfilment, she was past listening to good advice. None of the booking offices would accept her as a candidate for the Track, but on reaching Milford and spending a few days there she seized the opportunity of ostensibly making a little trip over to Sandfly Point with the launch one morning. That hurdle was easily cleared. Then there could be no objection to her going ashore for a little walk round while the boat was tied up at Sandfly, but once ashore she didn't look back.

She had plenty of money to supply the needs of a lifetime's travel and she certainly knew her way around. One hand was crippled, after a climbing accident in the Himalayas and subsequent lack of medical attention. Her physical handicaps and appearance were enough to excite the sympathy of the most hard-hearted, but not so her spirit, which was up to any demands. It was equal to the task of getting her to Quintin, apparently undaunted by the effort but, we wondered, would it be equal to the task of tramping over the Pass and down to Pompolona in the morning? My wife did not strip her bed linen, confident that she would be back to it.

Before she left in the morning this elderly venturer had a heart attack. "Oh my heart, oh my heart!" she exclaimed, clutching that region, but her heart, like every other interference with her plans, had to bow to her will. George Pollard, whose responsibility it was to get her there, with all the the conviction of one who knows and knows he knows, pronounced, "She'll never do it!"

George's gloom when he set off with her in the morning was enough to ensure the failure of the most hopeful venture in the world, but her hard shell was quite proof against it and it had no effect on her performance. When he returned he told us how she managed it. She took very short steps and, where she had to make an extra effort, never exerted herself beyond her strength. Many a similar performance by others makes one wary of pronouncing with certainty who is, or is not, in fit condition to walk the Track.

Another lady of a very different type came to spend a week or two at Quintin. She was the well-known author, Elsie K. Morton. She had in mind and in hand another book, *Fun in Fiordland*, with some of the characters in it drawn from the people she encountered on the Track. She wandered hither and thither, often barefooted, seeking material and inspiration for her book. The contact with her subject could not very well have been closer than that which her bare feet happily gave her, nor could she be more forcibly impressed by the facts she sought than by the roll of bacon which one day whacked her on the head. I had followed her into the storeroom, and in passing the bacon which was hanging from a rafter, she pushed it out of her way, pausing within reach as it swung back and caught her on the back of her head. She looked round so accusingly that I am sure she believed I was responsible and had done it on purpose.

As Easter approached we were sent an assistant from Milford. This young lady and a companion had also travelled in to Milford with us on the bus. When we met again and learned her name was Gladys Temple, I remarked, "A relation of Shirley's I suppose?"

To my surprise she replied, "Yes." Her father and Shirley's were cousins or second cousins, I can't recall which.

George Pollard followed Bob Gillespie as Pass Guide. Bob left before the season closed to go home to his father's farm at Riversdale, and George carried on to the end of the season. There was no telephone between Pompolona and Quintin and the numbers in the track parties usually varied from the lists compiled some time before the trampers left Te Anau. After several parties had followed in succession with swollen numbers, I asked Bob where he was finding these extra trampers. He had a farmer's ready answer with "the natural increase".

George didn't attempt an explanation but dealt with the situation in a more practical way. When there was enough sunlight, he flashed down the numbers in the party from the vicinity of the memorial cairn with a mirror. When old Sol wasn't co-operative, he would see the party on its way, dash down to tell us the number, then sprint away back again. Anywhere within a mile on the track, you would hear his "Halloo". He ran down to Boatshed from Quintin one day in forty minutes, a feat which no one has excelled since. No wonder that he survived Korea to bring back home a Military Medal. It would take a smart man to line up his sights quickly enough to catch him.

The 1950-51 season was hot and dry. On the November day we left home to go back in to Milford we were given a foretaste of what was to come. The sun blazed from a cloudless sky, bathing the countryside in a shimmering heat as we made our way up from Invercargill in the bus. The sheep in the paddocks we passed, while grazing, turned their backs to the sun, their bodies giving their heads some little shade from its rays. But we found the weather not so good at Milford and light rain persisted off and on the next day as we made our way up to Quintin. Before embarking on Lake Ada, Jack Sullivan started up a fire and left me to keep it going while he got the boat ready. Rain came on heavier and the fire took some tending to keep it going. With the fire going strong and the billy boiling when he came back, Jack remarked that my father must have been a Red Indian.

I remembered this when one evening I was called to tend the fire in the ladies' dormitory. All it needed was putting together when up it went with a blaze. Exclamations of surprise and approval tempted me to repeat, "Yes, my father was a Red Indian." Some gave a little uncertain laugh, and others looked at one another, not knowing whether to treat this seriously.

While getting Quintin into working order for the season, weather favoured us and we were well prepared for the first trampers. The biggest item again was the laundering. Some 150 blankets were not so easily handled in the primitive laundry and they took some drying on the lines.

Before the track opened, Wesley Grocott, an MOW engineer, came up from Milford on his way through to Glade House. As we had the work well in hand I rang up Mr Berndtson to see if it was all right to go through with Mr Grocott. He had no objections so we started off in rain which fell steadily but not too heavily for two days. We spent the first night at Pompolona then went on to Glade. I double-staged back to Pompolona the same day, still in the rain. The rain was not heavy enough to delay our passage beyond a few minutes here and there as we looked for a safe crossing at the creeks.

On the way down to Glade we stepped aside to look at the remains of the Three Mile Hut, burnt down earlier that month and with it its occupant Ike McCann, a very popular trackman and guide. Sandy Brown, foreman that season at Glade, had spoken to him on the phone the night before the fire, when all was well. He could make no contact in the morning so went up about noon to find the hut destroyed and the body positioned as if Ike had been overcome while asleep.

After an hour or two we were thoroughly drenched, and Wesley asked me if I had brought my bathing togs with me.

"No," I answered, "I didn't think I would need them when we had the Track all to ourselves."

"You never can be sure," he said, and I found that he was right.

Later that season, at Pompolona, Des Manning was kicked by a horse and had his leg broken. As contact could not be made with Te Anau, Mike Cassidy made a fast trip to Quintin to get word through to have the *Tawera* sent to the head of the lake. The afternoon was sultry and Mike, to cool down, plunged into one of the waterholes. Gathering up his clothes he sped along the Track while drying off. No sooner had he dressed again than along came two unheralded ladies on their way to Pompolona from Quintin.

Over the years Wesley's periodic tours of overseeing track installations have consistently been accompanied by rain. Repeat visits by many track patrons have been dogged by the same misfortune. In the Quintin Visitors' Book there is an entry, "Third time over the Pass, still seen nothing." One budding artist did a little better than that. Depicting "What I saw on the Milford Track", he drew a pack and legs below it which splashed along before him, all the way from Glade to Sandfly.

The third day, when I came back to Quintin, the sun shone brightly, the atmosphere was crystal-clear and the view from the Pass was perfect. Paradise ducks with their young were everywhere. All unseen, I watched for quite a while the performance of four very young ones, sailing motionless like leaves on the smooth surface of the water, or darting without apparent effort swiftly to catch a fly.

With the opening of the tramping season on 1 December, the track and house staff were brought up to full strength. Mr and Mrs Longshaw were in command at Glade and the Dohertys at Pompolona. On our side Oliver (Toot) Carran was track foreman; Gordon Craig, guide; Brian Blackie, packer; in addition to Nick Haggit and Pat Frampton. Frank Auld and my sister Julia were our household assistants.

The men on the track were keen photographers and vied with each other in looking out the best spot from which to take a full-length photograph of the Sutherland Falls. Their interest in this search had been stimulated by repeated requests from trampers to be shown where such a photo could be taken.

George Longshaw, during his time at Quintin, had taken a very fine full-length photo of the Sutherland Falls from a point above the bush on Mt Pillans and he sold prints of this at Glade House. Naturally enough, people would rather take their own photo than buy one, even if it is better than any picture of their own. They would hurry down from the Pass and ask where to go to get the best photo. It was a three-hour walk, and we would tell the few who were down early enough where to ford the river and point out to them the creek to follow which would take them to a spot beyond the intervening bush. On their way down the track to Boatshed some would climb the slope at the half-mile, just before reaching the rock bluff and get a good photo, but not a full-length one.

I was not a photographer, but a little of the enthusiasm of the others began to affect me and looking from Quintin it seemed to me that the nearest vantage place would be on Mt Pillans, directly in line with the lowest dip in the valley on the rise a half-mile from the falls. I went exploring and found a good view which took only a half-hour's climb from Quintin.

The following day I took my wife up and when we came near the place I had looked out she said, "It looks as if there should be a good view from up there."

"We'll have a look," I said, and we found it just perfection. The early afternoon afforded just the right light and shade and as May had brought her camera she took the first photo of the falls from that viewpoint. This shot, enlarged and framed, we had for many years in the dining-room at Quintin. It has since disappeared, the first picture taken from "Maysview" (the name I gave this lookout).

One evening shortly afterwards I guided most of the staff up to it. In the cool of the bright closing day, no time or condition could so favourably impress the party on its first inspection. On their arrival, the first view of the falls revealed in full splendour so affected the party that they seated themselves in silent admiration, nor was there a word spoken until half an hour later, when I broke the silence by saying it was time we were returning before darkness overtook us. The glowing sky, from the sun already set, the deepening shadows gathering round the silky ribbon of the lazily falling waters in the distance, the silence, stillness and overall beauty of the scene made it difficult to shake off the spell and tear ourselves away.

One day when Mrs Berndtson paid Quintin a visit and we took her up to the lookout she was so impressed with the view that she decided to recommend to the Tourist Department to have it opened up for the regular track walkers. The track I had blazed up to the view was known as "Bill's Track", but Mrs Berndtson declared it should be named Anderson Track.

To guide the trampers as they approached the lookout I put up the sign MAYSVIEW. Later that season when our daughter

Dorothy, son-in-law Jack Caldwell and son Arthur visited Quintin, Dorothy, looking around, found another lookout near Maysview. I put a notice up there too, DOROTHY'S VIEW. Later when full parties started using the track I cut away the growth which separated the views to allow more room, thus making them one.

One day as Toot Carran was making a wheelbarrow I approached him and said, "The barrow can wait. What about coming with me over the ground the track has to go to link up with the Falls Track?"

Nothing loth, he dropped his tools and away we went. We first went straight up to Maysview at a medium pace, finding it took us twenty-five minutes. We started off on a beeline for the Sutherland Falls, but finding the route hopelessly fierce, we went no further than the big boulder-strewn creek up which the photographers originally went for a photo of the falls. We then followed the creek down to the river and now changed our search for a track to a search for a natural bridge or a suitable place for one.

We found the river exceedingly attractive in its wild beauty. Waterfalls, cascades and swirling pools in the rocky, green, mossy ravine, shaded from the sun, were so near yet seemingly so far from the busy track. This was what we found instead of a bridge or a track. But this was all gain and would add lustre to the track we planned. We followed the river till just above Giant's Castle we found a tree, lately fallen, reaching out with its branches to our side. Thinking we may not find another safe passage we crossed by this tree and made our way through the bush to the Falls Track.

As we passed Giant's Castle it seemed to me a place worth another look but it was not till four years later when again I was looking for a bridge site that I explored its underground passages, waterfalls and dungeons. What I found amazed me as much as it has captivated and entertained so many people since that time. I thought that at some distant time a track would be put in to allow the beauty of this stretch of the river to be exploited, but so forbidding was the route I hardly expected to see it in my time. However, the few I took to see it were so impressed that I was persuaded bit by bit to improve access to it until full parties were eventually guided down that river track.

Toot Carran never got that barrow finished and every time I I saw it I was reminded of my interference with a good job.

When the trackmen came in at the beginning of the season they lodged in the men's dormitory. Their hut was in ill repair and due to be replaced. The timber for the new one was stacked under the dormitory awaiting the carpenters. The men were exasperated at the delay and when it drew near the time the first tramping parties were due, they very reluctantly set about putting the old hut in order and shifting into it.

This was the last remaining hut of the first two erected at Quintin in 1897. Its floor had collapsed in one corner and the rocks which lined the iron chimney, once firm and squarely built, were now in the habit of falling in on the fire. They declared the place was haunted by the spirits of the old departed pioneers of the Track. But it takes much more than this to depress the young, healthy, undeparted spirits and this old relic, in its last year of active service, saw more of merriment than of gloom. Trackmen's breakfast, sharp at 7.30, was an occasion of robust rivalry to see who would be first inside the door leading to the kitchen. Each man had to be seated on his bunk waiting for the buzzer to announce breakfast ready. As soon as the buzzer sounded there was a tremendous commotion in the hut. Often an odd limb would appear several times before a whole person gained the open. There again the wrangling would be renewed until one would break away to be pursued and tackled at the door. Here the final tussle determined who would be champion for the day. The race was not always to the swift or the battle to the strong.

The firewood this season was obtained from the slope leading up to Mt Hart, a hundred or two hundred yards from Quintin. Toot Carran rigged up a cable down which each load of timber came with a rush, spelter rising in a dust cloud from the wire and with a musical singing sound accompanying it. The stopper was a big old stump, but it began to wear away and let an occasional stick get past. These missiles were potentially so dangerous that a man was always on guard to warn the stranger. The Quintin staff knew to look out when they heard the wire tuning up. The laundry still shows a dent on the corrugated iron wall to the right of the door where one missile was halted on a twenty-yard flight. Some travelled as far as the men's dormitory, another six or eight yards farther on.

The season went quickly, as all trouble-free seasons have the habit of doing, but it was not altogether easy for the boatman and the packer. The river was so low that at times the stores had to be unloaded at the ferry below the rapids and packed from there by way of the ford above the boatshed.

The season was ideal for the house staff, as its chief chore, the laundering, was easily dealt with. Our assistants had their two days off, which meant that on four days out of the seven no more than three were on duty. In February, when the numbers coming through began to dwindle, Frank went on to track work.

I took the opportunity one day while he was working on the Falls Track to get him to help me measure the distance from Quintin to the falls. The distance was officially set down as one and a quarter miles, but so many trampers were sure it was longer that I thought a check would settle the argument. We found the distance exactly one and a quarter miles. After their big day coming from Pompolona, it is not surprising many of them find that mile and a quarter very much stretched out.

From early in the season Gordon Craig talked about climbing the face of the cliff alongside the Sutherland Falls. We didn't take him seriously and the bantering he got was enough to discourage a less determined adventurer. The day dawned, however, when he judged everything favourable for the climb. The first inkling I had that he had made the attempt was in the afternoon when Mr Berndtson rang from Milford to see if I had an explanation for the fire above the falls, reported by the pilot of a plane. I told him that probably Gordon Craig was up there. "Why did you let him go?" he asked. I replied that I was only guessing and that Gordon had said nothing about it to me that morning. When Brian Blackie arrived with the packhorses from Boatshed he told us that Gordon had told him that morning he was going and if he decided to come back over Mt Hart he would light a fire. By this we knew he had got safely there and would probably turn up before dark. Brian, Frank Auld and I went up to the falls and we could see the smoke from two places, one towards Mt Hart and what appeared to be a newer one near the falls.

We left Frank Auld to keep a watch on the face of the cliff from a quarter-mile back while Brian and I went up some distance to meet Gordon. The noise of the falls made calling futile and it was possible he could pass us close by and not see us on the lower slope, so after a time we rejoined Frank thinking that if he was on the way down he may have spotted him. Frank had seen no sign of any movement nor could we, as we carefully scanned the course he must follow. It seemed to us now that when at this late hour he wasn't in sight, he must be putting in the night up on top, so we made our way back to Quintin. Only a short time after we arrived back, we were sitting in the kitchen expressing our various views on the matter of Gordon's return, when in walked that gentleman. We were so surprised at his appearance, practically on our heels as we came from the falls, that for a moment we were speechless. Gordon hadn't anything to say either. We could see he had undergone a strain. He stood leaning against the sink and it was a while before he or we were ready to talk.

He had investigated the Mt Hart return route, but found a precipice an insurmountable barrier. He was unwilling to come back the way he went up, but his clothes were soaking wet and at the altitude, over 3,000 feet, the temperature would be low enough at night to make the thought of putting in the night there even less inviting than the climb down. He wasn't surprised we were not able to see him on his way down, for the bushes, which appear small from below, were mostly above his head as he slid down most of the way. He had experienced some bad moments when he hung by his toes to enable him to get a grip lower down and when he found he was letting himself down a 200-foot drop instead of ten or twelve. He told us he wouldn't tackle it again for £10,000. For some nights after this when he closed his eyes to go to sleep he would see this yawning precipice below him.

A climbing party at Milford was alerted and its members were preparing to come up to Quintin to assist in a rescue when I rang up to say that Gordon had returned. I think they were disappointed at being cheated out of an exciting adventure.

The dry season, with one long spell of nearly a month without rain, burnt up the moss on the rocks and it peeled off. Young beech trees growing in rubble began to wither and die. Freshly cut firewood with a day or two's sun on it burned as fuel ought to burn. I salvaged some rata from among the driftwood down the creek on the horse track and combed the nearby bush for broadleaf. These timbers helped to generate a bit more heat and saved coal. A big old dead beech standing just over the little creek at Quintin had a great crown of dry limbs which I hoped would break up into cords of firewood when felled. It proved as good as expected. In addition its trunk was so shaped that it gave Toot the idea of making a garden seat from it. Toot was born in the bush and was very clever with his axe. He soon knocked the seat into shape but the timber from the heart of the tree was full of moisture and tremendously heavy.

One evening after dinner we gathered to shift it to its place at the edge of the clearing, where it still invites the weary to rest. If we could have got together a team such as manhandled the *Tainui* over the isthmus at Auckland and had the benefit of the tohunga's incantations, there would not be much of a story to tell. Lacking experience in hauling canoes and garden seats over dry land and scorning the incantations, the marvel is not that there were some hitches but that we got it there at all. First it was manhandled from the stump across the creek to the open. So far so good, but the carriers got weary and looked for something a little easier.

The guests were now trickling out after dinner and forming a wide circle round the hub of business. I arrived as Brian approached with Blondie, the same horse we had met the year before. All I was concerned about now was to ensure a safe escape route when the fatal time came. The seat had already been levered on to the sledge, so all that remained was to attach the horse. By now there was a tight circle of onlookers. All they saw was a quiet horse and all they expected was a quiet leisurely plodding of the same to a place only two chains away. But what actually happened occurred so quickly they were momentarily rooted to the spot. Blondie, true to form, immediately the load was secured made a mighty plunge and a bound, but the circle held so he made two wide sweeps before a gap opened to let him escape. The track hands were new and didn't expect this performance from the quietest horse in the team. The seat of course immediately rolled off, and away down the horse track went horse and sledge, the latter spinning and somersaulting over and around each obstacle until coming to rest among the fern. The unfettered horse continued his flight and in a moment disappeared. Back to the ropes, crowbar and skids and the seat inched its way to the appointed place. As if to add refinements to this bizarre exhibition the architect of the seat marked on its back the date 31/2/51.

The season ended as it began, with rain. We made a rather hurried trip down to Boatshed and, warmed up by our exertions, felt all the more the cold wind on the river and lake.

There were rumours of the Track closing for two seasons but they were not substantiated till later in the winter.

9

REBUILDING HOTEL MILFORD

To AVOID INTERRUPTION in the work of rebuilding the Milford Hotel after the fire of February 1950, which destroyed the east wing, and to ensure the completion of the Homer Tunnel, the Track was closed for two years. During this time extensions and improvements were also undertaken at the Pompolona huts. All materials for Pompolona were packed from Glade House with ten horses. Mintaro Hut was started, and an attempt made to begin the stone hut on the Pass. But the Ministry of Works were not satisfied with the contractor, and they finished Pompolona and abandoned Mintaro and the Pass Hut. Dan Greaney and his gang were at work on the Track, mainly gravelling and eliminating corduroy.

Early in December 1950 I received permission to take a small party up the Track from Glade House to Quintin. The weather was not its best while we were at Quintin but was good on the way in and out. Snow had fallen the night before we left Quintin and was six inches deep on the MacKinnon Pass. Dan Greaney met us on the Pass as he was a little concerned about conditions there when we were due to return. Dan and the two or three others in for the season were stationed at Pompolona. Work went on through this season and the next on that side of the Track, but not on the Milford side.

Our trip, on the whole, had been a good one, but the last day was the most rewarding. The day was sunny and clear and the appearance of the Clinton River far surpassed anything I had seen before.

After her visit the previous season our daughter Dorothy had written to us in most admiring terms of the Clinton River, describing it as the most beautiful feature on the whole of the Track. At that time I had seen it only once and as it was in flood it was not at its best. I could not understand why she should praise it so extravagantly.

94

When we came in on our trip, the river at its normal flow was much more attractive and I too thought it the most beautiful river I had ever seen. But on our return, with the mists rising from its waters, coloured with every shade from glacial green to indigo blue, its beauty defied the choicest words to describe it. This display must be rather rare for only this once have I seen it in these gorgeous colours. Others who have walked by the river scores of times have told me they have never seen it as I described it.

It is not uncommon to see the mist rising on a sheltered river as I have seen it on the Arthur and on the upper reaches of the Pourakino, but never in colour as this day on the Clinton. Fred Muir, the well-known photographer of early times, who accompanied MacKinnon, McKenzie and Pillans over the Pass immediately after its discovery, wrote of the Clinton River: "The Clinton is the prettiest and grandest piece of river scenery I have ever come across and I have seen nearly all the rivers of New Zealand." It may be that he too had seen it as our party did on that bright December afternoon.

During the following autumn and winter, May and I looked after our brother-in-law's sheep run at Middlemarch while he with his wife and family made a trip to Britain. Upon their return in the spring we went to Milford to relieve Mr and Mrs Berndtson who were taking extended leave.

Milford Sound was bustling with industry, with plenty of interest and actual entertainment in watching the new hotel rise from the ashes of the old. I found that building an hotel, like the course of true love, doesn't run smoothly. The blueprints don't eliminate the possibility of changes in plans, the need for adjustments, nor do they act as referee in every dispute.

During our time there the weather was mostly fine and had settled to a regular pattern. Each day the wind rose in midmorning and fell in the evening. The early mornings were perfection with the smooth glassy surface of the Sound reflecting exactly the bush slopes on the mountains, their clear-cut peaks and the azure unclouded sky. The first gentle caressing touch of the wind led me involuntarily to turn my eyes to the Sound. Already the waters were ruffled, while away down near Stirling Falls a line of advancing white horses is on the way, galloping up to the head of the Sound.

The weather was all in the builder's favour. Tenders submitted on the basis of the average number of wet days give the contractor a welcome bonus when the weather remains consistently fine. Although the wind came up each day, it was not strong enough to blow away all the sandflies. We were in big trouble when one day the insect repellent failed to arrive with the stores. The reaction was as spontaneous, relentless and final as an avalanche let loose on Mt Pembroke and the echo as formidable, from the roar, "No Dimp! No work!"

At the close of his life an American millionaire declared that all the problems he encountered in the course of his career had a simple solution. Well, here was a problem, but where to turn for the solution was another. Eventually, Jack Craig, Neilson's foreman, came to me with a plan to raid the AA Motor Camp, a mile distant, and carry off the loot he hoped to find there. The AA Camp, like the Track, was closed for the duration of the rebuilding and the keys were left at the hotel. We went to the camp and found a dozen bottles of Dimp. With this rationed among the company, the hammers again rang out merrily, and the sandflies, out in force to take advantage of a day's good hunting, fell over each other in their hasty retreat. When Ivon Wilson, President of the Southland Automobile Association, paid Milford a visit I told him we had raided his premises and he congratulated us on our initiative.

I usually accompanied Cliff Rogers on his regular trips up to the Homer Tunnel for stores and mail. We timed our arrival to follow the day's blasting and before a start was made to shift the spoil. One time, before I went up to Milford, the truck arrived at the mouth of the tunnel and the blast blew in the windshield of the truck. Stores were brought in to the heap of rubble from the other side and we had to manhandle them over that obstacle which reached nearly to the roof. The lights from the headlamps of the truck illuminated the pile of rocks but not so clearly the ominous cracks round some projecting slab poised threateningly above us. One such ugly great piece I observed had quite a good healthy crack above it and, as I thought Cliff hadn't observed it, I said nothing until we had gone under it with the last of the stores. "Did you see that before we started?" he asked.

"Yes," I replied. "But I thought it just as well you shouldn't know till we were finished as we couldn't avoid going under it."

Office work was by no means exacting but the less time I spent there the better I liked it. The Berndtsons had a good vegetable garden, and with the good season, I put in some odd moments at it. Jack Craig came to me with some cabbage plants wanting to know where he could plant them. I undertook to dig up some ground alongside the west wing and planted them but had to put up protection from the persistent wind which would have killed them.

Surveys were being taken for the hydro-electric power. I went over the pegged line from the Bowen Track to the intake from the Bowen River and thought to myself, "There's some rough work here for the contractor."

The fine season brought the bush flowers out in bloom earlier than usual. This was one of the rare seasons when every rata tree was ablaze. Looking down the Sound the slopes of Phillips, Mitre Peak and Cascade Mountains were dyed red with the massed display.

One day my wife, while reaching for something from a chair in the bathroom, lost her balance, fell on the side of the bath and cracked a rib. Mrs Andrews, wife of the government overseer, a qualified nurse, made her as comfortable as possible and I took her home. I had to leave her in our family's care while I returned to Milford, and after the Berndtsons came back, about a week after, I took a run up to Quintin with the electrician, Derek Walsh. This was now January 1953 and we found the Track well overgrown.

The first major obstruction we came across was a tall heavy tree lying across Giant's Gate suspension bridge. It had broken the iron railing and depressed the bridge, taking up all the slack, but without any giving of anchorage, pylons or suspension. We pushed our way through the limbs, with the feeling that our added weight might prove the last ounce needed to drag it down to the bed of the creek. Clear of the heavy bush round Steep Hill, where the sunlight had full play, the Track was completely overgrown and in places we found it easier to make our way off the Track altogether. We followed the horse track across Mackay Creek and forded the river where at one time a chair was the means of crossing, and following it a bridge. Midway between Boatshed and Quintin, where slips during the war had denuded a wide area of vegetation and left a surface covered with rubble, growth was

97

G

now at the stage where makomako was springing up astonishingly fast and here we had to push our way through at every step.

We found Quintin in very good shape, with no sign of any visitors having entered since our visit the previous season. The next morning we were up early and set off up to the Pass, looking in at the waterfalls on our way. Thundering Falls impressed my companion as combining everything that makes the perfect waterfall. Size, he thought, did not count for so much if all else was pleasing. When we returned from the Pass Derek went up to see the Sutherland Falls while I, still with my mind on the continuation of the Anderson Track, made my way up to Maysview and then, following a course Toot Carran and I thought the most promising, I scrambled through the jungle on a sweep above the beeline. More by good luck than good direction I arrived at the river close to the place I had aimed for. This route had nothing to recommend it, and, with time enough for another scramble, I plotted a course that would take me a little below the beeline. This brought me to the 20-foot perpendicular bank of the Rena Creek. I followed up the creek then crossed at the first opportunity. From there to Maysview I went on a direct course which was above the line Toot and I had followed. This was as fierce as any ground I had covered and I was now satisfied there was no easy going anywhere and it was only a matter of keeping to a serviceable grade and picking one's way.

When I got down to Quintin I found Derek rattling up something for dinner and I might say I was ready for it. When we left Milford Mr Berndtson had jocularly told us to evict any squatters we found in occupation at Quintin. The only time in two seasons unheralded visitors had come they chose the very day we were there to meet them. Taking the official line that unauthorised persons on the Track should not use the huts, they were quite prepared to pitch their tent in the clearing. They had come over Dore Pass and were returning the same way after visiting the Sutherland Falls, and arrived shortly after I joined Derek. They were a pair of fine young gentlemen from the North Island and we were pleased to invite them in to share with us the shelter and comfort Quintin had to offer.

The next morning Derek and I made our way down the Track, enjoying every mile on this beautiful day. The Giant's Gate bridge showed a fresh crack across a plank on the decking which indicated the severity of the strain on it. We found our dinghy as we had left it and Derek, not satisfied with having rowed all the way over from Milford, insisted on doing the same on the way back.

We reported to Mr Berndtson, specifically mentioning the Giant's Gate bridge and the bridge over the Poseidon Overflow, a bearer of which was showing a decided sag. I suggested that something lasting should replace it. "Do you know how old it is?" he asked.

"No."

"Forty years," he enlightened me. I was not then aware of the lasting qualities of the beech that grew up there. The same species were not highly regarded for their lasting qualities in lower Southland.

First one stringer then another was propped up on that bridge and it was made to last for another twelve years. When I went in one season I found one side sagged so low I was afraid the next flood would carry it away. I got a winch and tried to lift it but where it was broken the ends locked and the winch made no impression on it. All I could do then was to prop it as it was, chop it through and raise each length separately. I would sometimes remark to passing trampers, "This bridge has a fifty-foot span, is fifty years old and your chances of getting over it without it collapsing are fifty-fifty." This was an exaggeration of course, for two of the heaviest packhorses, Prince and later Pepper, made unauthorised passage over it in its latter days.

After her accident, my wife's health began to deteriorate though this was not due to her fall, and in April 1954, after a steady decline, she died peacefully. We had hoped to spend some few more years together at Quintin. We had talked so much about what should be done and could be done for the interest, welfare and enjoyment of the people passing through but our partnership in this was now ended.

Apart from my own loss, May was to be greatly missed at Quintin where her cheerful competence and unflagging kindliness to many a wearied track walker were gratefully acknowledged in comments alongside names in our Visitors' Book. Her warm welcome and her prowess in cooking gave pleasure to all who met her.

With some hesitation I quote from our Visitors' Book a few samples of the appreciative remarks made by guests inspired mainly by her ministrations. There is nothing unusual in them as a perusal of the books in the reign of other hosts and hostesses will show, but they help us to understand what the tramper looks for and appreciates most.

"Your wonderful hospitality cheered our hearts." So runs a comment from a Mr and Mrs R. M. Young, Americans from California.

From an English traveller from York—"How could anyone not enjoy New Zealand after such kindness and hospitality!"

"This will do me!" from a South Australian visitor, and from a Western Australian: "Wild country outside but cosy inside."

Mrs Helen McCowan, Perth, Western Australia wrote, "Kindness is a gift which we receive here in abundance."

"A great oasis!" commented Hugh Brown from Scotland.

And from an English traveller: "Mr and Mrs Anderson's welcome and meal difficult to equal, impossible to better. A two days' stay that will remain a highlight of a three-month jaunt (round New Zealand). And the supper a memory forever."

Our own countrymen were no less appreciative. From Central Otago: "A wonderful welcome, and most comfortable place in New Zealand." From an Aucklander: "Would like to stay longer. Good food!" A walker from Invercargill: "Real Southern hospitality." An Oamaru comment: "I enjoy it more each time (my fifth trip). Mrs Anderson's griddle scones are really like mother makes."

Another Aucklander: "The hospitality and food as outstanding as you would find anywhere in New Zealand."

As I turn the pages of the Visitors' Book so many similar remarks are there. I remember Don Matheson of Otautau writing: "Mrs Anderson's hot tea and her smile are worth coming a long way for. And when I had finished eating, I had to go and sit by Mr Anderson's fire and not move. That *is* home comfort."

That entry pleases me even more than a short entry from a Northern Ireland visitor: "New Zealand wins."

For May and I had only one ambition: to show travellers from all over the world the glories of this part of it in as enjoyable an atmosphere as possible. We loved the place and wanted others to share our feeling for it. In our work, the comment that heartened us most came from Mrs Berndtson: "Great credit to Mr and Mrs Anderson for the friendly atmosphere at Quintin, and good food and cleanliness, but most especially for the new track they have made to obtain a perfect view of Sutherland Falls. I hope it will be always known as 'Anderson's Track'."

It *is* known by that name, but for May her walking days were over.

The Track had opened again in December 1953. On the Te Anau side of the Pass the track had been kept in repair but on the Milford side there was a lot of work to overtake. Mr Bonnington was foreman on the Milford side and Dan Greaney on the other. During that season Sandy Brown built the new trackmen's hut at Quintin. When the old hut was pulled down he found that some of the timbers had been cut in a mill at Tisbury. They were of white pine, none of which grows near Quintin, and were cut with a perpendicular saw, which only the Tisbury mill was using at that time. A hut for the manager and his wife was also built that season and the partition pulled down between the kitchen and the old quarters. This doubled the size of the kitchen and allowed room to work without treading on each other's toes.

There had been a plan, a very good one, for the housing of the whole of the house and track staff, but this was shelved.

Before the end of the season the Quintin couple walked out in much the same way as our predecessors the Smiths had done. Mary Christie and Barney Lang, the former general and Barney cook, kept the place operating efficiently until the season ended.

10

POLITICS

As I was involved in the 1954 Parliamentary Election I did not get in to Quintin till a week after the tramping season started, early in December.

I took part in Social Credit League activities, believing it would more quickly bring a knowledge of Social Credit to the general public. The threat of an up-and-coming new party would, I thought, induce the other parties to look seriously into the Douglas proposals and perhaps adopt its vital elements.

Some time before the election I rigged up my van with Social Credit propaganda and paraded the streets of Invercargill with slogans such as "Adequate money for peace as for war." "Wages are wages, prices are prices, and never the twain shall meet—till Social Credit comes." I held two meetings a night to cover the whole electorate, and at one of my earliest meetings I struck a man who, contemptuous of all political parties, attended meetings of them all to heckle the speakers for his own enjoyment.

I did not know there was someone in the audience ready to put me through it and I dealt with two or three interjections early on, after which I had a clear run of uninterrupted attention. The locals, who knew what to expect from him, were puzzled by his silence, but the reason was quite simple: I had converted him.

On election night we waited for results at our temporary headquarters in Invercargill. The first returns came from Awarua and votes for me were so pitifully few I felt oppressed with the thought that I'd let the whole cause down, but more encouraging returns came in, with Kennington, my home booth, being only one short of Mr Herron's National vote, so I perked up considerably. When finally all the electorates were accounted for, Awarua, though not successful, emerged as a bright spot in the Social Credit picture.

The *Southland Times* commented: "One of the surprises of the election was the votes cast for Social Credit in Awarua." In comparative percentages, Awarua came fifth in the Social Credit vote.

102

This optimism received a setback when, in the 1957 election, in which I again stood for Awarua, Social Credit slumped and I did not poll enough to save my deposit.

After the bustle of the 1954 election campaign I was glad to be back at Quintin. John and Ida Rawson were in command. Sandy Brown was again track foreman and Mary, his wife, whom he had lately married, continued as general, in the same occupation as last season.

Mine was a dual role, trackman, with Anderson Track as top priority, and assistant on the Quintin house staff. On the first day, I remember, I gave Sandy a hand to put up a harness shed. The old stable had at last become too dilapidated for active service and the horses were fed in the open. They might survive, but not their harness for long in this climate. Bush timber was used in the construction of the harness shed and old iron (very old and full of holes) four sheets deep to keep the stars from shining through and rainwater from entering, was applied to the roof. While this was still as stout and strong as ever eight years later, some philistines, with little regard for buildings of historic and artistic value, used it as a marker for a coal air drop. For no other reason than wanton sacrilege they chose it instead of the usual landing place on the soft ground in a patch of fern. The drop was as usual fairly accurate. One sack was driven through the wall of the shed where the iron was only one sheet thick, and another landed on the roof, which received a permanent depression, but sturdily shook off the intruder. The stable erected six years before was also in the direct line of fire and got badly shot up.

These air drops provided a welcome diversion at Quintin but it is as well the pilot could not hear the unparliamentary remarks when a parachute load settled down on the top of a high beech tree. On one run, when flying low, the plane plucked a branch off a tree and carried it all the way down to the landing place at Milford. Those trees which offended most were cut down, allowing the pilot to make a safer getaway after the drop.

One day unfavourable weather interrupted the air drop, but it cleared, and a trip was made unexpectedly in the evening. We were usually notified by phone of a drop and, if not, the pilot would make a preliminary circuit to give warning. Even with this warning there was no time to lose, for the horses, feeding then, had to be hustled away. As the plane came in we saw that this was no warning approach and shouted to those in the danger area. The horses had heard the plane and were off pell-mell down the track but the men were still in the target zone when down came a straight drop of timber. Some of it was smashed and one ugly big splinter hurtled close past Zygmunt Kepka like a javelin as he sprinted for safety. This was adding just too much spice to these diversions, which were diverting enough without an odd drop landing near enough to make the spectators scatter like this.

Some very accurate shooting led John Rawson once to challenge the pilot to land a coal sack square on the marker, which was a white sheet spread over clumps of fern. Several landed alongside, shifting it, and one skipped underneath carrying the sheet away, but John's ruling to "howzat" was "no score". On the last run but one the sack landed fairly and squarely on the centre of the sheet and the pilot collected his reward, a bottle of whisky. Popeye Lucas in his book, *Popeye Lucas: Queenstown* states that the sack slipping underneath landed on a corner of the sheet. This was not so, otherwise John would certainly have allowed it as "a hit".

My duties at Quintin followed my accustomed pattern. First on the list was the washing copper to light at six o'clock in the morning, the engine-room and all its works to attend to and the ablution block and the dormitory fires.

A week or two after I came in, I found the wood-burning grate belonging to the boiler furnace when looking in the loft above the engine-room for some timber Ivan Latham needed for repair work. I had not known it existed, nor indeed that the heater was designed for other than oil fuel. Without dismantling the diesel furnace I experimented with the grate and wood fuel. From stone cold it heated up in two hours, a very satisfactory performance. As Sandy was agreeable to the change I turfed out the old and installed the new. We now had hot water day and night instead of a service limited by the available fuel.

Second growth had encroached upon and almost reached the building on the side next the engine-room, and Sandy told me to clear a strip back a half-chain or so and use the wood in the furnace. This I very willingly did and the provision of abundant hot water for the ablution block was hailed as the greatest thing that had happened to Quintin for many a day.

December and January are busy months and I did not get much time to look at the Anderson Track, but as soon as I could I made more exploratory sorties on that side of the river. I first had another look at the river to see where a bridge could most easily be put across and where it would best serve the track. Going up beyond the point Toot Carran and I had reached, I found a very nice waterfall. I cut a track from it on the Quintin side to the Falls Track, intercepting it on the rise a half-mile from the Falls. I took Sandy and Mary up to see it one evening and asked Sandy to name it. He did so, giving it his wife's maiden name of Christie. As she was the first lady to visit it the name was very appropriate. Sandy timed the walk from it to the Falls Track, and found it a mere three minutes.

At the edge of the heavy bush, two or three hundred yards above the Christie Falls I found the ideal place for a suspension bridge. It had everything I wanted for anchorage and supports so from that point I started to blaze a track by the most direct route and easiest grade I could find to Maysview. I armed myself with an old sheet, tore strips from it and tied them to twigs where they could be easily seen as I went over the line again.

I didn't do any blazing or cutting until I was fairly sure I was on the right route. I had to go a number of times over the stretch between the river and the big Rena Creek before I was satisfied it was in the right place. To take advantage of a suitable crossing, higher up the creek than I expected, I had to accept a steeper grade but compensated for this by making a milder one between the creek and Maysview. This is the most difficult section, and I wandered a number of times over it, frequently led off the course by the roughness of the terrain and the indirect route I necessarily followed to maintain an even grade. Finally, tiring of such slow caution, I chanced keeping to the approximate course and, beginning at Maysview, slashed my way to Rena Creek and came on to it a half-dozen yards from the intended crossing.

I have been asked scores of times how to go about finding or making a new track through dense bush. The answer I think is that there are no two tracks exactly alike, and the method will vary with the natural guides. If I can get an overall bird's-eye view of the area before starting, that is half the battle. There are ridges and creeks to guide on sloping country, and an approximate keeping to the grade prevents me wandering too far from the course. Some people have a built-in direction finder and always know where they are and where they are going. Others find it a job to keep to a ready-made track, let alone trying to find or make one. A new track is generally developed in three stages, first the blazing, then the cutting and finally the forming.

From an engineer's point of view I made a retrograde step when I changed the site for the bridge. Public opinion, as expressed at Quintin, declared that the bridge should be erected at Christie Falls where the scenic qualities of the river would outweigh advantages claimed for the other site. At Christie Falls the river plunges down under huge rocks and when the river is at normal height, goes out of sight altogether. From the bridge one day I watched two blue mountain ducks fighting in the river just above the Christie Falls. All they could do was grab each other by the bill. It seemed to me that by these ineffectual means the fight could go on all day without a decision, but so engrossed were they that they failed to notice their drift to the top of the falls, where the current suddenly gripping them, swept them down and out of sight under the rocks. I didn't expect them to drown in this underground stretch of the river but waited to see how long they would be in reappearing. It was ten minutes before the first one appeared and the other shortly after. They seemed to have forgotten then what the fight was about.

The rocks under which the river flows form a natural but rather precarious crossing. On this bridgeway I made a ladder of twisted wire and wooden rungs. I was not too keen about using it myself at first, with the fall spitting at me on one hand and a deep drop on the other. I could very well then make allowance for the distaste for this device when, near the end of the season, I guided some of the early arrivals round the track.

On one of the first parties, an Aussie girl, confronted with this proposition, exclaimed in dismay, "Have I got to go up there?"

"Yes," I replied, "or retrace your steps right back to Quintin. But if you do go up you will be the first lady to have done so."

She needed no further urging but was up and over it like a squirrel. I kept a tally of the numbers going round the track on that last month of the season and they totalled exactly one hundred. Beside these, many during the season went up to Maysview and back to Quintin before going up the old track to the falls. Of those I guided round the track, I would take a few, when there was time, down to see the Giant's Castle.

The acrobatic feats demanded on this jaunt seemed only to increase their enjoyment. I was well rewarded by their appreciation of what they saw and felt confident that work put in to make it more accessible would be well justified. One young fellow told me he had been over all the hunting ground in the back areas and broken new ground without encountering a feature equalling the Giant's Castle.

When I came in off the track about 5 pm on the day the last party for the season came in to Quintin, I found a hue and cry raised for a missing tramper, a Sydney girl. There was a chance she might have missed the turn-off to Quintin and gone on down the track to Boatshed or she might have gone up to the Sutherland Falls without first coming in to Quintin. These possibilities gave only slender hope and it seemed she was still somewhere between Quintin and Crows' Nest from which point two of her companions, after a brief rest, set off, leaving her to follow. Sandy Brown was guiding that day and following the party down from the Pass overtook the three girls at Crows' Nest Hut. At that stage they could not be expected to come to any harm and Sandy went on to see how the others were faring. Sometimes the leading members of a party may be approaching Quintin before the last leave the Pass and it is possible to give individual attention only to the few that need it.

Sandy was preparing to go back up the Track as I came in, and I followed after I got the engine going to provide light, and stoked up the furnace. At Roaring Creek I met Sandy coming back. He had gone as far as Moraine Creek thinking it possible she might have gone back for something left behind or inadvertently retraced her steps as some have done. A track may look very different going back over it and it has temporarily fooled a number of trampers. On one occasion two ladies left the track to go in to see the Camp Oven Falls and upon returning set off back the way they came, reaching Doughboy before they realised their mistake.

It was now getting dark and we were becoming really worried. As we made our way down the track we gave a halloo at each creek that crossed the track, but got no reply. Care was needed in crossing some of them where a false step might end in a slide of considerable distance with serious injury at the end of it. Presently we saw a light approaching and John Rawson with the information that she was not on either the track to Boatshed or on the Falls Track. It was John's theory that she had wandered off the track at Roaring Creek, but there was the other possibility that she might have fallen into the creek at one of the waterfalls. John and Sandy went on down while I went up the Track again to Roaring Creek. The bed of Roaring Creek is about two chains in width with big rocks and boulders strewn over it. With my torch I criss-crossed it from the base of Mt Elliot down to the abrupt drop at the cascade. I thought it possible that missing the track on the Quintin side she might have wandered up or down and falling among the rocks be lying there injured. With the thought of the earlier tramper who disappeared without leaving a trace I felt it would be a relief to find her even if she were seriously disabled. I had just completed my search when a light appeared and Claude Hamilton hailed me with the good news that she was found. Claude and Lawson Burrows coming up the track gave a halloo at the creeks as Sandy and I had done but with better fortune for they got a faint reply. There was a precipice down which it seemed risky to descend so Lawson went back to Quintin for ropes and more help.

On unfamiliar ground there is a big difference between a pitch black night and daylight. I myself was not so familiar with the place at that time but felt there should be no great difficulty in reaching the floor of the valley. I had a good torch and approaching the cliff at first glance saw only a black void but, edging nearer, found sufficient foot- and handholds to climb down. Calling now and then to keep near the voice down below, I eventually came to her.

And now, immediately the quest was over, reaction set in, a lassitude came over me and in a leisurely manner I looked for an easier way up than I had come down. Betty (for that was her name) said she had wandered about till dark, and, having heard that there was nothing to be afraid of in the New Zealand bush, settled down for the night and had actually slept for a while. The night was mild, but a faint fog was rising from the valley and at that altitude (2,000 feet), it would be a little chilly by morning. We made our way yard by yard up the almost vertical slope but with plenty of handholds there was no danger. There was nothing to guide us but an occasional exchange of shouts with Claude, which, however, seemed to come from no particular direction. As long as we kept climbing we must come to the Track and at last we did so, some distance lower down from the point I left it.

We had not gone far down the Track to Quintin when we met the rescue party. They brought some dry and liquid stimulants which were gratefully accepted by the rescued and should have been by the rescuer. But now I felt queasy and was sure I couldn't swallow a grain. Betty thought I was holding back on her account and insisted I should share the biscuits. To please her I resigned myself to the consequences and nibbled at a chocolate biscuit. As I expected the effect was instantaneous but with a different result. With the first taste I felt as right as rain. All that was wrong was an empty stomach for too long; I hadn't eaten for twelve hours. I had put in a hard afternoon's work and was working more or less under pressure while the hunt was on. We got in to Quintin at 12.30 am and soon made short work of the substantial dinner reserved for us.

I went up next day to see the course Betty had followed to take her where we found her. Missing the track she had wandered down the creekbed to where it drops into a gorge, then on the steep, shrubby bank had continued on to where there is a sheer drop alongside the Veil Falls. Bushes grow on this cliff face and by them she had let herself down to the valley floor. The night was still. Had there been a breeze to rustle the leaves or rain to deaden the sound of the call she might never have been found, for there is a much larger area to get lost in between the creek and the Track than appears, and the likelihood of her making her way down there had seemed to us the day before very remote.

The most likely places are naturally examined first and the seemingly impossible places are often left till too late or not searched at all. At an early time when the Track was walked both ways, one lady, on the way back, went down off the track to have a closer look at the Lyndsay Falls. Instead of returning to the Track, she then carried on across the river above the falls and got lost in the bush. They looked for her from about noon, and as the day was drawing to a close a searcher fancied he heard a voice across the creek as he passed the falls. He dismissed the matter as fancy, but after reaching Quintin he knew he would have to prove this otherwise he would get no rest. With others he went back to investigate this most unlikely place and she was found, but in a very poor state and had to be nursed back to health.

In the 1890s, when the Track was open to anyone who cared to go over it and when it was optional whether a guide was engaged or not, a number of people were found by the Ross brothers in similar straits to that poor woman.

The 1954-55 season closed. It had been full of interest and I looked forward with pleasure to the next.

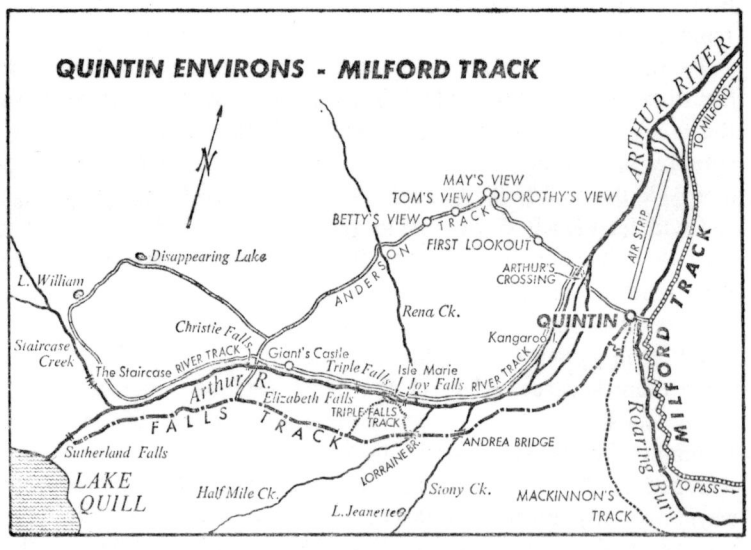

11

A PIANO FOR QUINTIN

I WENT IN TO MILFORD with Sandy early the next season but we did not start work on the Track till the beginning of October as we were busy in general cleaning up work at the Milford Hotel. The last of Sutherland's buildings, an old cottage, was demolished and a site prepared for the new staff quarters. Before going over to the Track we put the telephone line in order between Milford and Sandfly by erecting a new pole at the low water island. The pole at this point often had to be replaced for it had to stand up to tide, flood and driftwood from the Cleddau River. It was a race against the tide in the little while it was out, and digging was slow among the rubble.

When we eventually shifted over to the Track, Sandy was occupied with some carpentry at Sandfly while I went up the Track cleaning out the watertables. We then concentrated on clearing the telephone line and removing fallen limbs from the Track.

At Labour weekend we went out for a few days and I now made preparations to carry out a long considered plan to take a piano in to Quintin.

While we were there during our last season together May had missed her piano greatly so in an off-hand way I had promised that if we returned I would bring one in. Although not really in earnest when I made that promise, the idea grew in my mind. She had been as keen as I once we emerged from fantasy to reality. While there was still prospect of going back to Quintin, the attractiveness of the proposal grew while the difficulties of its accomplishment diminished. Not only for her own pleasure but for the tremendous boon it would prove for staff and guests at Quintin, she had been excited with the thought of the fulfilment of this day-dream. Although the dream did not materialise the idea survived and, having plenty of time to revolve it in my mind, I realised that the notions my wife held about the use and value

111

of a piano at Quinton were still valid. Consequently, at the close of the 1954-55 season, on my first call to Invercargill, I found the very instrument I was looking for.

I knew it would get some knocking about on the way in so I looked for a secondhand piano, but as far as performance goes, as good as new. I had the whole winter in which to make my choice but in Todd's room of musical instruments right at the door was one, the tone of which made an instant appeal to me. It had not been greatly used and was in impeccable order mechanically and otherwise. I knew at once this was the one for me. I had not the slightest desire to look at another and there and then bought it.

Sandy Brown, my son Bert and I spent an evening talking around the problem of getting it in, weighing all the hazards, and in our minds tackling in advance the tough places on the Track. The plan we considered most workable was to take the piano in without dismantling it and to have it well padded in its case.

Two pairs of flanged wheels, their axles clamped to the bottom of the case, would provide locomotion. They would run over Dexion angle steel rails, ten feet long, made into three sets braced together. Each set, as the piano moved over it, would be shifted and placed in front. In this leapfrog fashion we calculated two miles could be covered in a day. We all agreed that transport should be designed not for speed on the easy going so much as to meet conditions on the worst sections of the Track and, as the labour force was uncertain, with the fewest possible operatives. I put together the sections of rail track while I left Bert to cut the flanged wheels from the rollers of an old caterpillar tractor, and get the whole outfit ready for the road.

On my return to the Track I spent time eliminating some awkward places, and early in December, Bert brought the piano in on his truck, put it aboard the launch skippered by Jim Aitken and landed it in the afternoon at Sandfly Point.

By a coincidence a dinghy for Lake Ada started off on its journey up the Track on that same day. It was loaded on to the old Milford firecart, mounted on a pair of rubber barrow wheels. Over the first mile the going is good and the boat's crew were well pleased with their effort when they cast anchor a little more than halfway at the close of the day.

The Park Board Huts at
Lake Mintaro.

Mackay Falls.

Ray O'Brien at the base
of the Sutherland Falls.

Up near Christie Falls.

LEFT: The author at Qui
tin.

BELOW: Ray O'Brien wi
some members of the 200
party he had guided to tl
Pass.

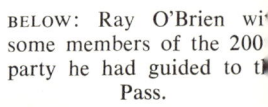

A Piano for Quintin

I came down from Quintin, caught the Ada boat and reached Sandfly at 4.30. There I found the boat's company gathered round the piano while waiting for the launch to leave, and lively talk in progress on the merits of this or that mode of transport. From the varied opinions expressed there seemed to be general opinion that ours was not the most practical way of getting a piano up to Quintin.

Shortly I said to Bert, "Right oh! Now we know how to get it there we'll make a start." With a last glance back as we disappeared into the bush, we left the others still engrossed in the subject.

Sandy, who directed the boat's crew, camped at Sandfly and asked us to dine with him in an hour or so. This we did, then on our way to Doughboy where we lodged, we pushed the piano another few hundred yards and covered it up for the night. The next morning we were up at about 4.30 and before we went down to Sandfly for breakfast, pushed the piano to a spot beyond the boat.

In answer to his query how we got along with the piano we told Sandy we had got it "up the track a bit". We thought we would give him and his team a surprise when they found the piano nowhere in sight.

John Rawson was mightily interested in what he called the piano-boat race and from Quintin was ringing up all the places down the Track for a progress report.

We reached "Little Annie", the hill at a mile and a quarter, with some misgivings, but just as we were about to tackle it, a party of plumbers and carpenters arrived on their way to Quintin, and with their aid the piano was whisked up to the top with barely a pause. We worked away quietly until presently Jim Downey the boatman overtook us. We were now within a half-mile of Doughboy and, as there was no need to rush the job, Bert suggested we take a spell and go down to see how many knots the boat was making. To our surprise it had not moved at all. Sandy's team had celebrated only too well the success of the previous day and Sandy, like a model captain, had not deserted his vessel. But now, with no hope of getting up steam and raising the anchor, he transferred his support to the other competitor, the tortoise. With his help we leisurely trundled it along to Doughboy.

113

This eventful day was made still more noteworthy by the arrival of Mr and Mrs Edgar Williams from Christchurch. They came over on the launch in the evening and, borrowing a packhorse to carry their camping equipment, made their way to Giant's Gate Falls, from which they made their assault on Terror Peaks the next day. Mr Williams and his father before him are so well-known in the annals of mountaineering that any comment I could make on their prowess would be superfluous. Both father and son were well-acquainted with the Track from its earliest years and used it as a springboard to accomplish many notable ascents. Mt Wilmur, that sharp peak between Mt Balloon and Mt Elliot, embraces the names of Williams Jnr and Murrell, who were the first to climb it.

The weather was still good, and gave us the opportunity to ship the piano to Boatshed. Arriving there we found the work party which had rendered such yeoman service at Little Annie returning from Quintin, and ready to help get it off the boat and up into the safety of Boatshed.

Here I heaved a sigh of great relief. The job was now as good as done. We had proved the mobility of our device and left behind the water stages, which could have given a load of trouble. All that remained now was patience and hard work, but no insurmountable obstacles to meet. We had been very fortunate in getting the piano up the lake and river when we did, for the day it was shipped was the last trip the big boat was able to make because of low water. The dry weather lasted with few breaks for the remainder of the season.

Blazing hot weather in January put the temperature up to, and on some places on the Track, beyond 100 degrees. At the halfway mark between Boatshed and Quintin there was a narrow, winding, rocky path to be bypassed to allow the piano to get through. Here the sun, in this sheltered spot among the rocks, had it all its own way. The fuchsia leaves hung like rags from the branches and it was not until about mid-afternoon that the faintest breeze stole up the valley to fan the air. Sandy Brown shot the rocks impeding the way, while I bridged the creek and scrounged round for surfacing material to make the bypass presentable. Not since playing round on the Egyptian desert with a full pack had I lost so much sweat, but it was worth it to see the finished job. Rough spots like these were relics of the wartime devastation. The fine season allowed much track improvement to be made and it cheered us to hear Mrs Berndtson say at this time on her visit to Quintin, that the Track was in better shape than it had been for years.

I didn't want to move the piano from Boatshed until there was a good chance of getting it quickly up to Quintin. More help from track hands became available after about a month's interval and reinforcements arrived from home. My son Jack, with Jack and Dorothy Caldwell, son-in-law and daughter, ensured that at least a scratch team was available. A three-man team took it about a mile and a quarter from Boatshed where a full team was ready to take over. For this full team we needed one at each corner of the piano, and one for each set of rails. From Quintin we had four miles to walk to reach the piano, and the two Jacks and I, making an early start, got it near to the open stretch of Racecourse Flat by the time the rest of the team arrived. John Rawson and Dorothy, in addition to the team, kept ahead, so that at intervals a cup of tea and a snack was available. It was very encouraging to see the smoke ahead and to anticipate this welcome breather.

Our progress seemed to us satisfactory enough, but to our caterers we seemed to be galloping along, hardly giving them time to get the billy boiling before we were on them again. We covered Racecourse Flat in astonishingly good time. On the long straight stretches the railsetters had the hardest time as there was the briefest rest between the "lay down" and the "take up". The piano pushers soon became so adept that they didn't wait for the sections to be exactly fitted and, except for sharp bends, could keep up the pace as fast as we could put down the rails. In rough going, packing (a piece of rock was usually available) was needed to support the rails, as the timber support two by one and a half inches was not heavy enough to span a ten-foot depression. Across some of the creeks and depressions we would superimpose one set on the other to give the necessary strength. A big boulder that we could not avoid could usually be negotiated by allowing the rail section freedom to operate in a see-saw fashion.

We reached the top of a rise between the two- and three-mile sign, getting over a hideously rough piece of track with a hairpin bend round a huge rock before leaving it and calling it a day.

The next day no track hands were free but my two Jacks and I pushed the piano three-quarters of a mile in the afternoon. It was now only one and three-quarter miles from its destination but

115

Gentle Annie was there to dispute our passage. Many had declared this hill would prove our Waterloo. Jean, Jack's wife, who went to Quintin when the piano was taken in to Boatshed, said when she saw this hill, "They may get it this far but Gentle Annie will beat them."

If the half-ton weight (including case, packing and transport attachment) had been an object that could stand some knocking about, it would have been much easier to handle and to move quickly. We couldn't allow it to get any bad jolt, overturn or run away from us on a slope, and there were plenty of opportunities to do all these things before Gentle Annie was reached. Now we had to exercise all the strength and care at our command.

This last day started with a drizzle in the manner which so often slowly develops into heavy rain. We waited to see which way the cat was going to jump and when, at about 10 o'clock it was getting neither better nor worse, we decided we would give it a go. We had to leave the piano covered, which added noticeably to the weight we now knew so well. Sandy Brown now came in to help as he had on the first stretch at Doughboy. With his extra weight and length to propel from behind when in motion, and to prop during a pause, we made a steady ascent without trouble.

In spite of the drizzle, which kept on until early afternoon, our catering team was back on the job to provide the necessary stimulant to reinforce morale and muscle. The most apprehensive moments during that notable day were spent on the short but steep descent from the top of Gentle Annie. All our hopes, all our labours and all our care would be in vain if, on the last major obstacle, we failed to control its movements and allowed it to crash on to the rocks. Once that danger was passed we felt the piano was as good as home. Another three-quarters of a mile over comparatively level ground was all that was left to cover, but now reaction set in. While struggling up the hill our strength was equal to the task and we felt no undue strain but now, on the easier going, the sense of accomplishment induced a listlessness and we mechanically, rather than purposefully, trundled along home with our prize. We were met at Roaring Creek by Ida Rawson and Mary Brown who had temporarily left preparation for a victory dinner to cheer our final spurt up the straight to the door of Quintin.

A Piano for Quintin

There were apprehensive, questioning looks as the case was opened, and I wondered how much it had suffered on the journey by road, water and rail. "What if someone has taken it out and put rocks in its place?" I wondered.

This comment was met with such horror that dire consequences might have ensued had not the next moment revealed the object of our concern, a little knocked-about but in surprisingly good condition. It had played a tune now and again on the way when it got a severe knock, but amazingly it did not need tuning. It had been tuned twice in the course of the few months since I'd bought it, which gave it every chance to hold the pitch. The springy rails eliminated severe jarring, and the care taken in transit fully justified the method employed in getting it there.

With the piano, a "first time" was recorded. In Rawsons' Visitors' Book Jack Anderson, whose place in the team was at the front of the piano, wrote against his name, "The first man to walk up Gentle Annie backwards".

Citing those who directly or indirectly had taken part in the undertaking, John Rawson made the following entry in the Visitors' Book: "January 23rd, 1956. A momentous day in the history of Quintin Huts. A piano, donated by Mr W. Anderson was this day delivered to Quintin, manhandled thirteen miles from Milford by the combined efforts of W. Anderson, John and Ida Rawson, Dunedin; Alex and Mary Brown, Te Anau; Jack and Dorothy Caldwell, Roslyn Bush; Jack and Jean Anderson, Kennington; Bert and Nola Anderson, Kennington; Peter Howard, Papakura, Auckland; David Swain, Karori, Wellington; S. J. Murdoch, Invercargill."

In addition to these were Jim Downie, Lake Ada boatman and Jim Aitken, Milford launch-master who played an important part, while the ready help given by the carpenters on their way to and from Quintin was not forgotten. The encouraging attitude of Mr and Mrs Berndtson of Milford Hotel, the help of Sandy Brown and the whole-hearted support by members of my family, made possible a venture that otherwise might have daunted me.

I wanted to give the piano a good reception, so in case there were no musicians with the first party (a rare happening we found) I persuaded Jack and Dorothy to wait. It was with great satisfaction we found that there were several good pianists and we were treated to a first-class musical evening. Evenings such as this in

117

the years that followed never failed to remind me that we were repaid a hundredfold for our toil.

This was not the first piano to go on to the Milford Track. In 1925 one had been brought up to the head of Lake Te Anau, taken off the launch at the wharf and rowed up the river to the old Glade House in a dinghy. This was a heavy instrument and must have caused its transporters many an uneasy moment while it was on the water. It perished in the fire which destroyed the house, so had a short, but we can well believe a merry life, in its three brief years.

12

TWO BRIDGES AND PASS HUT BUILT

THE WORK PUT IN ON THE TRACK smoothing the tough spots for
the passage of the piano was not wasted. All this was necessary
for the maintenance and improvement of the Track. Track-wise
as he was, Sandy was aware that this dry season was unusual and
took full advantage of it. Eliminating one by one the worst sections,
he finally concentrated on the long-neglected Gentle Annie and
surfaced some of the rough stretches. Midway to Boatshed, where
the track runs close beside the river, he did similar work. With
still some other places marked down for improvement, he and
Mary towards the end of the season left the Track to go to their
new house at Te Anau. On this section they have built their well-
known Matai Lodge.

Sandy had all the knowledge, experience and qualities found in
the ideal track foreman, while Mary in her sphere was equally
endowed and the track suffered a real loss in their departure. I
was given Sandy's job of head track hand, while Betty Paton, a
friend of Mary's, came in her place.

During the season Lloyd List from the Government Tourist
Head Office in Wellington came through the Track and suggested
that I might map the Anderson Track and send the map up to
Wellington. This I did piecemeal at odd times when I could
get someone with a little time to spare to take the end of the
tape. Mary Brown gave me a hand with the Triple Falls Track.
When Toot Carran and I first saw this waterfall from the left bank
of the river we reckoned it could be seen better from the Quintin
side. Without preliminary investigation, an hour's work cutting
through the thick fern brought me right on to the spot and, as I
expected, I found the falls made a beautiful picture from a big
rock in the river. After jotting down the necessary data from which
to make the map, I said to Mary, "We'll have a look at that wee
island down there in the river."

The river was low, and by stepping from boulder to boulder we reached it dryshod. I then said to her, "You go on to it first for you will probably be the first person to have done so."

I named it "Isle Marie", a variation of her name. After going out at the end of the season I finished my map of the Anderson Track and sent it to the Head Office.

Early in March Betty and Harry Caldwell, my daughter and son-in-law with their three children, Robert, Ian and Joy made a surprise visit, coming in from Milford. Joy was only four years old and, as I have seen so many little children do, flitted along the Track easily. After reaching the cairn on the Pass, still as fresh as a daisy, she asked her mother, "Do we go on up there?" pointing to Mt Hart. I have kept the little pair of boots she wore as a souvenir.

One beautiful day I took Betty, Harry and Mary up the far side of the river from Quintin as far as Christie Falls. As Betty and Mary were the first ladies to visit that part of the river, I gave my daughter's name, Elizabeth, to the waterfall a little above the Triple Falls.

I had profited by working on the Track with Sandy, and after he had gone I tackled some of the jobs he had planned, as I felt that anything he had recommended would prove successful. One of these, referred to by Sandy as the mudhole, was a two- or three-chain stretch between two of the creeks midway along Racecourse Flat. This was a relic of the great wartime slips. A mixture of tree trunks, stumps and rocks with water running over and oozing between them made this the worst spot on the whole thirty-two-mile Track. The packhorses sank up to their knees, dragging one leg after another over obstructions. It was so bad that a bypass was made for foot traffic earlier in the season.

While the water was running, the job of cleaning it up was almost hopeless, but the continued dry season had now, for the first time, stopped the flow. I pounced on it before the rain should come and shovelled, chopped and blasted to remove the major obstacles from the Track and to provide a channel to divert the water. As it consolidated I surfaced the track with gravel barrowed from the creeks.

From the worst, this was now equal to the best section of the Track. In the absence of a full maintenance staff it is only in this piecemeal fashion that the Track has been attended to in recent years. A process of deterioration can be found on one section, but when there is a more urgent call to another it must wait, and while waiting deteriorates even faster.

The next job on the list was the widening of the Track at the bluff where it touches the creek a half-mile from Quintin. I blasted some rock away leaving the Track, if not good, then at least less hazardous than before.

Ken and Jean Bigwood paid the Track a visit during this season and I accompanied them on some of their jaunts. They made a good coverage from Sandfly to the MacKinnon Pass. Photographing for the Film Unit, they collected material for the well-known picture *Four Ways to Milford*. When Ken found that the waterfall seen from the bridge at Quintin had no name he named it Ida, after their hostess, Ida Rawson.

Their superb photograph of the Sutherland Falls, taken from Maysview, Anderson Track, appears in many books and tourist publications. Sad to say, a picture framed by the branches of the beech tree as in that one can no longer be taken. Some vandal in the 1968-69 season wantonly cut down a tree that made this ideal framing. Judging by the childish manner of its felling no regular track hand could be blamed for this desecration. Another small tree, a kamahi, has also been hacked about and left with little chance of survival.

The Pass Hut, erected in 1928, was blown down for the second time in 1947 and lay there with its four walls and roof separated but still intact. The promise of a new hut, renewed yearly, had not been fulfilled. The day I was up on the Pass with Harry, Betty and the youngsters I scouted round and found the door of the hut a considerable distance down the slope. Stoutly built of oregon timber, it wasn't much damaged, so as it seemed nothing of importance was missing, I thought I might try to put the pieces together again. The floor, well anchored, was still in place. Some of the studs on the wall frames were rotten, and these I replaced with timber brought from the bush a mile away, and pretty crooked stuff some of it looked alongside the straight sawn timber. I wired each section of the wall, one to the other and to the floor, then planned to slide the roof up a ramp into its place. For this I gathered a party, six strong. The roof was twenty or thirty yards away and when we came to shift it we found we couldn't get any movement out of it at all.

The roof was made of heavy arched angle steel with heavy-gauge roofing iron, overlaid in the middle with plain galvanised iron. Yet this heavy unit had been tossed by the gale like a leaf from a tree. I think some unauthorised person had visited the hut and left the door open, a fatal omission where the wind, pressurised against Mt Balloon and higher ground on the Pass, races through this gap with hurricane force. With the door open the hut would fill like an overtaxed balloon and explode. We stripped the iron off the roof and left only three steel rafters. We were then able to slide it up the skids and anchor it to the walls. At this stage there was no time to lose as everything had to be made tight before the next hurricane.

In the early stages of the work I camped down at Crows' Nest, in the valley near Roaring Creek. I found it saved time to prepare my meals while I worked at the hut and went down only to sleep. The early mornings and late evenings were at times indescribably beautiful. In the calm clear evenings when I had finished work and the keas quietened down, a hushed silence seemed to steal over the whole region. The gathering gloom in the Clinton tried to oppress the senses, while the roseate hues of the setting sun on the Jervois Glacier and more distant heights elevated them to quiet, serene exaltation. The shadows deepened as I made my way to my crib. Can there be a dimension beyond the realms of this overpowering beauty, silence and peace? What is the ultimate in our capacity to respond to, and contain, a greater fill of such rich fare? These questions arose for my mind to play with at the limit of its vision.

One evening I left for Crows' Nest later than usual. As the darkness gathered, the mountains too seemed to close in around me. As if it felt I was out of my element and needed company, an owl accompanied me most of the way down from the Pass. Where there is movement we expect sound, but in its flight from shrub to shrub or from rock to rock, not one whisper reached my ear. Later at night he could of course make plenty of noise with his "more poke". Near Crows' Nest I could hear the kiwi at any hour of the night and the kea was always ready to take over from him at the first glint of dawn. The kea's first call actually appears frequently to be an attempt to mimic the kiwi. With the sound of my hammer in the morning each kea would increase his screeching tenfold.

As soon as the hut was habitable I spent the nights there. The cold was intense, and I arranged my cooking utensils alongside the bed so that I could prepare breakfast and have it before I rose. Up and dressed, I had to work furiously to keep warm. My hands at times got too cold to hold the hammer.

I had the company of a score or so of keas, a pipit or two, a weka and a stoat. I never saw the latter but until I got the building tight it came in looking for eggs. I thought at first my count wasn't right but when I found he was taking one each night I promptly put a stop to his little game.

No gales came until the hut was ready for them and only one night have I spent there when a real howler came along. I had seen what the wind could do at Middlemarch, in Central Otago, but this eclipsed anything I had experienced. There was a continuous roaring. My bunk was against the windward wall which buckled inward with the terrific pressure of the gusts. I wouldn't have dared open the door a fraction of an inch, and as for going outside, I felt that whether on my feet or not I would be whisked away into the Clinton Valley.

Early in the season Sandy Brown erected a suspension bridge over Poseidon Creek. Working from Boatshed, he and his assistants, under considerable difficulties, made a first-class job. The bridge was put to very severe strain a few seasons after when two freak floods, following closely one on the other, did considerable damage to the decking. It was repaired and is in as good shape now as when first erected. Now at the close of the season we had another to build. This one was on the Arthur at Christie Falls. After the last party and staff had gone from Quintin, Peter Howard, Neil Barns, Stan Murdoch and I remained to do it. The weather had worsened and a cold dribbly rain made working conditions miserable. But this was the last job before going out, so we all worked with a will and so well that we had the bridge up in four days. This bridge eliminated the chief obstacle on the Anderson Track, and with the good work accomplished elsewhere we could look back on a most successful season.

During the season a survey was made for a hydro plant to serve Quintin. The intake was to be immediately above Lyndsay Falls, and the powerhouse would be put across the creek from Quintin on the upstream side of the bridge. We had little expectation of this scheme materialising, sound and good as it was, and when we came back in the spring Peter Howard, Pass Guide, made this comment in the Visitors' Book: "Just before we left we took down the line posts to make the clear ground available for a helicopter to land supplies for the hydro in the winter. Ha! Ha! Did the helicopter come in, and did the hydro scheme get started?"

13

EMERGENCY TRACK REOPENED

THE 1956-57 SEASON, before the opening at the beginning of December, was plagued with persistent rain, not heavy, but enough to get us wet after an hour or two's work on the track. With the rain the snow frequently came down below the bushline.

For convenience in crossing the river at Boatshed I brought in with me a light plywood dinghy. For want of a boat, work on the track at Steep Hill and beyond had been sketchy, so we now took the opportunity to upgrade it.

The few weeks we put in there were, I think, the most miserable I have endured on the Track. We soon exhausted our wardrobe of dry clothes. Our old stove had enough to do keeping itself warm let alone dry our clothes or disperse the dampness and chill in the building. I went up to Quintin for some old rags I had left from the season before, but now when we were about ready to move on, there was an improvement in the weather.

Before we left for Quintin I had a look over the ground between Boatshed and Mackay Falls and it seemed that, with the aid of the dinghy, we could take trampers to see the Mackay Falls and Bell Rock. Before the tramping season began, I cut a track across to Mackay Creek, felled a tree to make a crossing and again put on view these beautiful features which for almost a half century had been passed by. During the previous season Bill McIndoe, who was stationed at Boatshed, had taken advantage of the unusually low water to ford the river and guide a few trampers across to see them, and their delight in Bell Rock and Mackay Falls left us in no doubt about the wisdom of opening a way to them.

Ray Kelly, who had gone in with me early in the season, was for this and some following seasons stationed at Boatshed to cater for the trampers at lunchtime when on their way to Milford, and to ferry them across the river. The cargo boat had to be hauled through the rapids and, with plenty of work on the Track within reach of Boatshed, Ray became more or less permanently established there. At that time rapids at the entrance to Lake Brown gave a lot of trouble, but some seven years later the riverbed altered, and they practically disappeared.

With everything going satisfactorily at the lower end of the Track I was able to concentrate on the upper, between Quintin and the Pass. When the Track was formed there in the late nineties, MacKinnon's Track which did not cross these creeks, was kept open for use in any emergency when Roaring and Moraine Creeks were impassable. It served this purpose until the First World War when it became overgrown and was not restored. Those who knew the route no doubt made use of it at a later time, for it is not difficult to find a way over. Slips in times gone by have swept the surface clean over wide areas, and bush has returned to clothe it but not to impede passage over it. It seemed to me that it would surely be easier for parties to come down to Quintin by this old route than to retrace their steps to Pompolona when the creeks were too high to cross. Mr Berndtson agreed but wanted no more time spent on it than necessary to make it reasonably serviceable. I left the project with Peter Howard, Pass Guide, to put through, with occasional assistance from others. With other work claiming attention the new track took shape very slowly.

When Peter Howard scouted round to find traces of the old track from Beech Huts to the Pass, he was able to follow it for about a quarter of a mile, but after that only here and there, where a little formation had been done at the approach to some of the creeks. Near the junction of Roaring and Moraine creeks a big beech which had fallen across the track had a section cut from it to allow unimpeded passage. It had evidently been left some time before the crosscut was put through it, for there was still evidence of a bypass round its trunk.

Between Moraine Creek and the Pass, for about 200 yards before emerging from the bush, the track plainly ran in company with the telephone line, long out of use. From the bushline to the Pass, MacKinnon's Track followed a course some distance down the slope from the present route and passed by Lake Ella on its western side. No forming was attempted and its approximate position can only be determined by studying the old survey maps.

Before working on the old track we had uncovered the site of the Beech Huts. I noticed a short section of formed track leading away from the Falls Track, some two or three hundred yards from Quintin, and followed it up, clearing the growth which completely enveloped it, until I came to the top of the rise where old tins and bottles showed that a hut had been there. Fossicking about, I found a levelled place, but covered by fern and decaying tree-tops, the remains of timber cut down six years before by Toot Carran for firewood. After clearing this and the fern away I found first a fireplace, and then the exact outline of the spot on which the hut once stood.

A channel cut round the outside of the walls to lead the water away marked perfectly the hut's position and also its doorway. Right in the middle of the fireplace grew a goodsized common fern (*Polystichum vestitum*). I hauled it out and found a quite sound tin matchbox caught in its roots. Numerous brass ends of fourteen-gauge cartridges indicated the extent to which the native game had been used to supplement the larder. Among other interesting relics I found two coins, a threepenny bit and a halfpenny.

Another fireplace marked the position of the other hut, while additional levelled spots would probably have accommodated tents. In his diary William Quill describes the preparation of the site on which Donald Sutherland's hut was re-erected, and as it took some digging and levelling it would, I think, be the one on the side of the slope with the channel round it. Here I wanted to build a replica of the old hut, which both Donald Sutherland and William Quill had worked on, and use it to house the many relics of former days, but I never got round to doing it as there were so many other jobs to do.

As we pieced together the story of the old Beech Huts, MacKinnon's Track, which we were reopening, grew in significance and in interest to both the staff and visitors. With pressure from other necessary track work, however, it had to take second place and it was not until the next season that it was linked up with the Pass Track.

The 1957-58 season surpassed all previous records for rainfall, with 334 inches recorded at Milford. The rainfall at Quintin could possibly have amounted to an average of an inch a day during the tramping season, for it is heavier then than in the winter and normally a little above the rainfall at Milford. February clocked up sixty-nine inches. The dampness invaded the innermost recesses of every building. Linen put away dry in the cupboard would be

126

brought out damp. The piano, we found when we came in, had wintered well, only the top note being a little sticky, but now as the season wore on and in spite of constant use, its action was never entirely free. The continuous, heavy rains, while ruinous to the Track, prevented the carrying out of any useful repairs, and in the job of getting the trampers through safely the guides had to call for additional help from the track staff.

The last party to be turned back to Pompolona before the Track was completed got into difficulties on their return. They were held up between creeks for a considerable time and could neither advance nor retreat. They finally had to cross over the avalanche ice bridge at the head of the creek at Pompolona and in the darkness got lost in the bush. They did not reach the shelter of Pompolona till 12.30 in the morning.

To ensure that nothing like this should happen again we quickly finished the track, and before long had the satisfaction of bringing the first party safely through. Before the tramping season opened, the main track had been put in reasonable shape. The short track up the Quintin side of Roaring Creek was also improved and a viewpoint at Thundering Falls made safe with a railing. John Rawson had pioneered this track taking odd ones up to see the Ida, Thundering and Lyndsay Falls before a track was made. From this track, a much more impressive view of the falls can be seen than from the main track on the other side.

Carpenters, with Arthur Robinson in charge, came in early before the camping season. Two additional rooms were added to the staff hut, one for the track foreman. To allow room for the piano it was at first thought that an alcove would be sufficient, but this plan was altered to provide an extension big enough to hold additional tables and room for guests to move around. This to my mind gave a better return for outlay than any other improvement during my association with Quintin. A second sitting for meals was no longer necessary and this was a welcome improvement for the guests as well as a great saving of time for the staff.

In the extended dining-room people could group round the piano for a singsong. Here the piano escaped the almost unavoidable knocks and scratches it received in the right-of-way alongside the table. Pianos seem to be singled out for mistreatment. During one winter some deerstalkers stripped the coverings off the piano, left them lying on the floor where they and their dog shed the grime from their feet, took the plugs out from under the pedals allowing the mice free access, and for good measure left the keyboard open. They added further refinement by going through the song book clipping out the pieces that had taken their fancy. During the season the piano is well looked after but one time a young lady, to see what was going on at the other side of the room, jumped on a stool which supported one bare foot while the piano keys supported the other. She was a good medium-heavy weight and the tune she played was no "Kitten on the Keys".

A porch, long overdue, was put up at the entrance, where dripping waterproofs could be hung, instead of making a sloppy trail the length of the dining-room and through the dormitory to the ablution block. A safety exit, another overdue requirement, was made at the same time from the women's dormitory. A change, but of doubtful improvement, was made by the abolition of the open fires in the dormitories and the installation of space heaters in the dining-room and women's dormitory. The open fires held a great attraction for the guests, where they could rest and relax in comfort after their tramp. An Australian couple who had been through the Track some years previously kept reminding their companions of the treat in store for them when they reached the beautiful fires at Quintin, only to find that their party was the first to greet the space heaters.

The open fires had served a good cause in turning into ashes the rough trunks and stumps of trees close to the Quintin buildings. There was now only the furnace of the water heater left to digest this type of fuel and, to meet its demands, I next tackled the second growth jungle which grew close to the kitchen door. This tangle had generously accommodated and conveniently hidden a half-century's accumulation of an unbelievable variety of junk, very little of which was of recent origin as all waste was now properly disposed of. The thicket, growing through a knee-deep strata of bottles, rusting tins and wire, seized these by its roots and incorporated them in the trunks of the growing trees. The sight revealed beggars description. Here was the headquarters of the sandfly menace, and, in a different climate, would have nursed many a plague. The patience of Job, the determination of Quintin MacKinnon and the hardihood of Ned Kelly was called for to make a speedy job of it. Lacking in any great measure these qualities, I

'ows' Nest. A group of track walkers accept a cup of tea from the author.

George Wiseley, the first candidate for the new track up the spur of Mt Elliot, with the author.

The highest point on the Track. It should read 3,600 feet, not 3,500 feet.

LEFT: The Sutherland Falls and Lake Quill.

ABOVE: The airstrip at Quintin. The contractor was W. Connelly and Rex Smith was the first pilot to land on it.

LEFT: The airstrip at Quintin. Looking up Green Valley from MacKinnon Pass.

BELOW: Mt Elliot, Jervois Glacier and the Pass Hut.

worked at it at odd times when I was in the mood and gradually I whittled it away.

To make room for the extended staff quarters the woodshed had to come down. A small temporary one was put up, but in the moisture-laden atmosphere the wood, instead of drying, got mouldy and waterlogged. It burned best when freshly cut and taken straight to the stove. Such fuel would drive most cooks to distraction, but here we were given another example of how in the scheme of things, one extreme is balanced or cancelled by another. With the hopeless firewood, we had a magician as stoker and chef in Charlie Meggit, who knew the burning quality of every tree found in scrubland and in the forest. Time and again I would make apology for the condition of the wood, but never once did I hear him complain. The meals were always up to time and in addition to the normal catering he baked a variety of sweet breads. Added to his prowess as a chef, his genial disposition and reliability were qualities which made him highly esteemed alike by strangers and friends.

The first person to go over the new track up to the Pass was Rena McDonald who was on the Quintin staff. To mark the event I gave her a choice of the waterfalls on Moraine Creek to name. With her fiancé, Claude Hamilton, she made a choice and, that both should be associated with it, they named it "Hamilton Falls".

Claude was packing that season at Quintin and previously had packed on the other side at Glade. He held the record at that time for the fastest time made on foot between Pompolona and Quintin. Claude and Rena are now happily married in Christchurch.

When I looked over the ground the new track would follow, it was a revelation to me to find a succession of beautiful waterfalls and cascades on Moraine Creek. At about this time I attended the wedding of a young lady who had been on the staff at Quintin. On my return I carried on with the survey, and discovered two more waterfalls farther up the creek. These I named after the bride and groom, Margaret and Kenneth. Between the Kenneth and the Hamilton Falls the creek tumbles down over a number of ledges making a most striking and beautiful display. This I called the "Douglas Cascade", inspired by Major Douglas of Social Credit fame and as it followed the Margaret and Kenneth Falls it appropriately included the maiden name of Margaret's mother. The next waterfall to the Hamilton is the Canadian Falls. This name was

I

given by two Canadian girls spending a few days at Quintin before the season opened. They had shown a vivid interest in all they saw, one of them staying a night all alone at the Pass. They photographed all the Moraine Creek waterfalls and as one was unnamed, I gave them the opportunity to name it. I thought they might have named it Mary Anne, as one was Mary Lou, the other Anne. However, they were loyal to their country and would entertain no other name than "Canadian".

The next fall is hidden in a deep, narrow, rocky gorge. Falling halfway down the rock wall in a solid, perpendicular column, it strikes a ledge which diverts it to an angle corresponding with the hour hand at four o'clock. This timepiece display naturally suggested the name "Four O'Clock Falls".

The last in the group of falls I named "Linwood". This name was suggested by my daughter Dorothy, in recognition of the part played and interest shown in the Track by members of the Caldwell family. Linwood is the name of the Roslyn Bush farm whence in due course they one by one found their feet to settle within the boundaries of Southland.

Those waterfalls are not seen to advantage from the side of the creek the new track followed and it seemed a pity that such gems should remain hidden. With each viewing from the right bank I felt more compelled to make them accessible to at least a few trampers eager and able enough to make the extra effort. Bit by bit, I managed to do this.

As a sample of old Hewe's (Maori rain god) extravagant behaviour this season, the trees I cut down to bridge the Mackay Creek were in turn washed away. Contemplating my next move (there were no more trees available to use in the same manner), I was asked one evening at dinner what I had lined up for the next day.

In an off-hand manner I replied, "I am going to finish the emergency track, the following day put a bridge over the Mackay Creek and the next, go down to Milford to celebrate."

This boastful utterance was received in the manner it deserved with scornful "Yeas".

I had still to find a place and get the materials to bridge the Mackay Creek. As for Milford, I would need a much better reason for going down there. Spoken in jest, my words, however, actually came true. I did cut the last remaining link on the emergency track

on the next day. The following day I went down to Boatshed, got
Ken James to go over with me and we managed to do in one brief
day what could have taken a week. We found a leaning tree, some
ten feet or more above the creekbed, and we spanned the remainder
of the distance with two saplings as heavy as we could conveniently
manhandle into position. With some planks we got from Boatshed
we made decking. The trunk itself served as the other half of the
crossing. We anchored the bridge where it rested on the bank, but
until a good flood came along we were not sure how it would stand.
Although lightly built, it stood for six years before needing repair.

This bridge, the only one of its kind on the Track at that time,
was considered something of a curiosity. Novel features like this
take the fancy of trampers and it is the great variety of both man-
made and natural showpieces that puts the Milford Track in the
forefront of mountain trails.

I was back that evening to Quintin in time for dinner. Although
I had fulfilled my promise for the first two days, Milford still had
no place in my thoughts. I found, however, that Wesley Grocott,
Ministry of Works engineer, was with the party which arrived from
Pompolona and, as I wanted to consult him on some matters con-
cerning the track, particularly the Poseidon overflow bridge, I
went on with him the next day down to Milford. I had thus fulfilled my forecast to the letter—even to celebration in my usual
manner.

Throughout this quite abnormal season, we felt well repaid for
our effort in restoring the little old hut on the Pass. Rain down
below in the valleys frequently meant a blizzard on the Pass, for
the difference in temperature between Quintin, 830 feet, and Pass
Hut, 3,500 feet, ranged round 20 degrees.

Buffeted by the wind, drenched by the rain and sleet, the poor
abused travellers would stumble into the shelter of this haven for a
brief rest. To make room for their fellows they must without undue
delay scoff up their lunches and get out again into the storm.
At times they would pile into the hut long after it seemed there
was no room for any more.

One time they were jammed in so tightly that I got separated in
my corner from the teapot and could only hold up a cup of hot
water when another hand would appear to relay it to an unknown
destination. It didn't matter much if the beverage failed to tickle
the palate, as the cup's chief function was to warm the hands.

131

Those who were ready to go had the greatest difficulty in extricating themselves, for the late comers were between them and the door. My comment on this scene may bring to mind Dante's *Inferno*, but it differed in this respect, that the situation engendered hilarity rather than sighs and groans.

Track walkers almost without exception are true sportsmen and sportswomen and when things get tough their spirit rises to triumph over their plight. One day when a dozen or so had arrived looking sorry for themselves, having waded more or less all the way from Pompolona in the rain, one of their bedraggled number remarked that in the last letter from her mother she was reminded to make sure she didn't let her feet get wet. This advice, greeted with ironic laughter, provided the spark that spontaneously drove out self-pity and restored life and gaiety to the party.

On numerous occasions this season, snow fell on the Pass and four times reached down to Quintin, on one visitation to a depth of four inches. Two feet of snow was the limit we thought parties should be taken through. Just before Christmas five feet of snow fell on the Pass. When two parties were turned back from Pompolona Ken James and I went up to see what conditions were like on the Pass and only because I knew the area were we able to get to the top. I thought I would try to go over to Pompolona and see what was cooking there, but before I got to the highest point on the Pass I was floundering in drifts that seemed to have no bottom, so needed no persuasion to retrace my steps.

On the whole the parties came through the snow very well. The commonest complaint was chafing round the ankles. This, of course, could have been avoided with suitable footwear, but many came through in complete ignorance of the likelihood of encountering snow.

The new Pass Hut was now at last on the way but it was not till 21 November that it was completed and ready for the 1958-59 season.

14

NEW PASS HUT

BUILDING MATERIAL for the new Pass Hut, prefabricated in Invercargill, was air-dropped on the MacKinnon Pass near the end of the season in 1957. We put down a marker on a handy spot to retrieve the goods, but found its hard surface too damaging so shifted it to a gully, on the edge of which the hut was to be built. Each load was recovered as it fell and stacked away to save it from damage by the next drop. One bag from a load of gravel landed in the little tarn close by the hut and for a while puzzled us where it had vanished to. It wasn't in the lake and it hadn't skipped out of it as similar articles are apt to skip on land. After hunting round awhile we found a bulge in the tough peaty turf some two or three yards from the water and digging down through this, recovered the missing sack, none the worse for its submarine voyage.

We brought our lunch up from Quintin expecting to be back at the usual time for dinner, but the job wasn't over till night was coming on. I myself intended to spend the night at the Pass, but used all my stores in providing a scratch meal for the party, so I had to go down with the others. Darkness overtook us as we neared Crows' Nest, and my torch lighted the way for the now more careful footsteps.

A few days before this I hadn't been so fortunate, as darkness overtook me half a mile from Quintin. I was carrying a saw, hammer and axe, which were no help when I made a false step. I wasn't expected back, but John Rawson, on the chance I might return late, came to meet me with a torch. Surprise, pleasure and gratitude, I don't know which was uppermost when I greeted my rescuer.

The new hut, when finally up, proved of much greater service than the old one, which in comparison appeared like a matchbox in size. But it had given good service, and none greater than its role as a refuge for Sandy Brown while building the new. I had made

133

the old one fairly cosy and many times it gave overnight shelter to those keen individuals who wished to see the Pass in its morning glory. Once three girls with limited time to spare tried to cross the Pass. Rain came on and the shades of night came down sooner than they looked for them. Fortunately a guide met them, and built a fire in the hut and this, burning brightly all night, kept them warm and dried their clothes.

The new hut, so much larger than the old, still proved too small and at a later time was enlarged. Bob Johnston, aided by Patone Hekewaikarehakera, was entrusted with this addition.

The 1957-58 season ended the long association of Mr and Mrs Berndtson with Milford Hotel. As host and hostess none was their peer. Every branch of their managerial responsibility was shouldered with confident ability and marked success. In trying situations their patience and fairness won a remarkable response and co-operation from both staff and guests. Their knowledge, experience and commonsense equipped them to handle any emergency with competence.

Where the Track was concerned, Mr Berndtson had the uncanny gift of seeing what was wanted and knowing what was going on, without setting foot on it. While he was in charge I felt all would be well with the Track and I was sorry indeed when the time came for them to depart.

In August 1958 timber for a new wharf was shipped up to the head of Lake Te Anau and the Brown brothers erected the substantial structure which serves today.

Between the demolition of the old and the erection of the new wharf, two horses were brought up on the launch and were pushed off into the lake to swim ashore. The first one made a good landing, but the second promptly went to the bottom. While the crew were still staring blankly at the spot where it disappeared it come to the surface inshore blowing bubbles mighty fine as it plodded along the lake bed to dry land. When they came to cross the river at Glade the other horse swam while this one again hoofed it along the bottom. It seems sheer misfortune for this horse that he, perhaps the only non-swimmer in 10,000, should be sent to so watery a region.

During this season Sandy Brown put up a new suspension bridge over the river at Glade. This is the third bridge at that site. Official comment made on the workmanship displayed in the erection of the first bridge ("Good work has been done here") could well be repeated about the third.

Coming in to Milford in October, 1958-59 season, with Ray Kelly, I made a start on leading a track from Sandfly Point down the water's edge to the Lower Landing. From the river this stretch of shoreline looked rather forbidding, but Ray and I had given it a look over at the end of the previous season, and thought we had a fair chance of getting the track made before the tramping season. I had another dinghy of my own there so I would have no interruption in my work. There was a real need for this track for at low tide there is not enough water for the launch at the jetty and trampers had to get there by dinghy. Near the end of the season in 1940, while a boatload was being taken to the launch, the dinghy struck a snag and one man fell into the river and drowned.

We had two wide stretches of water to bridge on this track, and near the lower tying-up place a huge overhanging rock, washed at its base by tide and stream, barred the way. The inlet at the point holds dead water, and to bridge it I cut down a big old rough beech, and we rested the bearers on its limbs. The next stretch of water was flanked by a perpendicular cliff but at low tide the site was briefly above water level. At this spot sandflies really showed what they could do. They seemed to take this interference with their special breeding place as a deliberate insult. We got some of the heavier timber for this bridge from away up above the cliff. Work was slow under these conditions, but finally there remained only the big rock to deal with. By this time Ray was working his way up the track putting the telephone line in order and clearing away fallen timber. Time was getting on and there was still much to do before we were ready for the season's opening at the beginning of December.

The big rock had a lower section opened up a little by cracks, and because of this weakness I expected that this great overhanging monster could be dealt a successful blow once it was sufficiently undermined. I was able to place the charges quite effectively, and shot out a great quantity of rock, but still the main mass remained as at the beginning. Above this shattered section I was working on, it seemed flawless, otherwise the fifteen-foot overhang must have made its weight felt. I had no further time to spare, so when a passage through could be made by stooping I left it to attend to more pressing work, and recommended that the Ministry of Works should drill from above and bring it down. This was not done till three years later and many uncomplimentary remarks were made about the inferior treatment given on the last few yards of the Milford Track. But this unfinished job was at least appreciated by the launch-master, Graham Hayter, and the boatman, Barney Lang. Barney declared this was the biggest improvement made to the Track for many a year.

Later in the season I put in some work at Moraine Creek and improved the track leading from Crows' Nest Hut down to Moraine Creek and following it to Linwood Falls. The next season I made a link with the main track, crossing Roaring Creek 100 yards below Veil Falls. My son Arthur worked on this track with me, and Zygmunt Kepka named it Arthur's Track. I later put a bridge across Moraine Creek a little way above Margaret Falls, linked it with the emergency track on the Pass side and with Arthur's Track on the other.

One day as I was working on this track, some trampers turned down from Crows' Nest and I asked them if they would like to see the new piece of track. Anything novel, anything new, always excites the interest and curiosity of the tramper, so they willingly followed. Beyond the bridge there was a narrow but deeply-worn watercourse, hidden by fern, but spanned by a ribbonwood growing horizontally over it. One of the girls, Elaine Morgan from New South Wales, fell off this tree crossing and disappeared through the fern. If she was hurt at all, her glee at finding her camera safely reposing on her outstretched frame instead of damaged on the rocks, made her feel more pleasure than pain.

The Tourist Hotels Corporation was set up in 1955 to administer the government tourist hotels. It inherited the Milford Track along with Milford and Te Anau Hotels from the Tourist Department.

Track certificates were first awarded this 1958-59 season, giving the tramper written proof that he or she had actually accomplished the feat. The first presentations were made in the foyer at Milford by the new manager, Hans Gfeller. Humorously he extolled the glories of the Track and laid special emphasis on the three easy stages described on the certificate. It was evident by the fresh, fit appearance of the party, he remarked, that none had suffered any ill effect from the thirty-two mile walk. To show there was another side to this rosy picture, the first tramper called to receive his certificate approached Mr Gfeller with a run-down attitude and a most exaggerated limp.

It was soon found not altogether satisfactory to present the certificates at Milford, as some members of a party lodged at the AA Camp and others at the hotel and it was not so easy to get them all together again after they had separated. The certificates were therefore presented at Quintin. Although the trampers had not completed the journey at that stage they had reached the point of no return, so perforce could not do otherwise than qualify.

Until he came to know the Track and its needs, Mr Gfeller left its oversight in the hands of his second-in-command, Derek Surridge. During this season all went well for Derek knew his job and had the welfare of the Track at heart.

This was the last season John and Ida Rawson presided at Quintin. With the exception of the 1957-58 season they had directed the affairs of "The Huts" since 1954, quite a long period in hut management as the records will show. To gauge the worth of the service they gave track patrons we need not look further than the Visitors' Book. With an alert mind John had a zest in life which followed him in all his undertakings. John was in charge of the hotel during the off-season in the winter of 1959 and was especially praised for his heroic work in helping to put out the fire which destroyed the kitchen and dining-room. His death on 24 September 1967 seemed hard to accept when it appeared he had many years of purposeful living ahead of him.

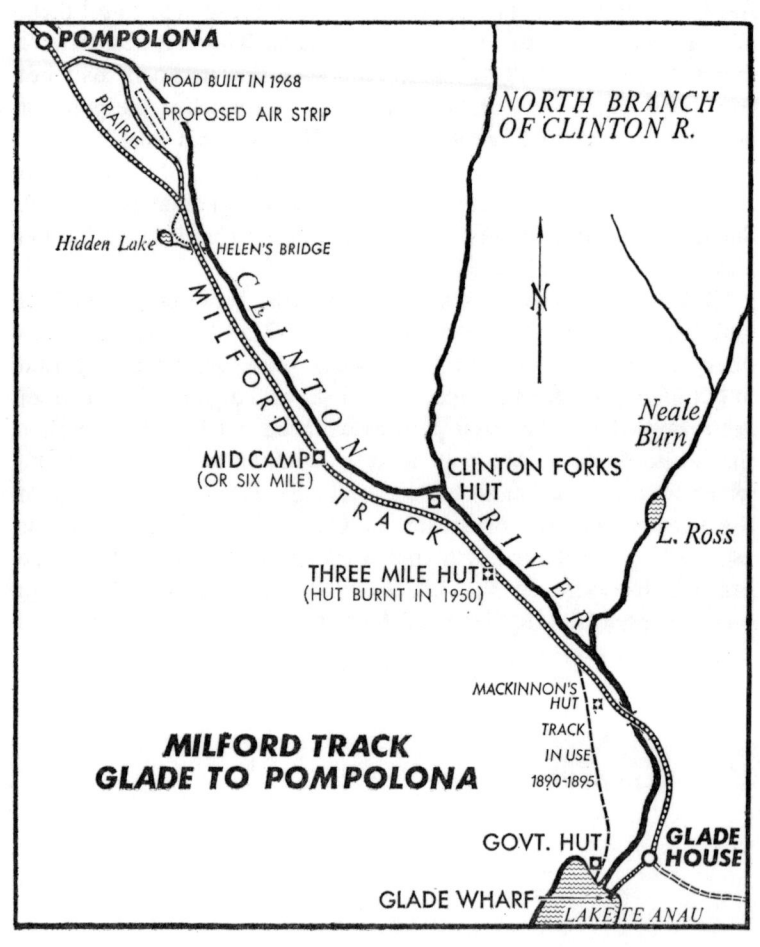

15

SECOND FIRE AT MILFORD

THE BEGINNING OF THE 1959-60 SEASON began dramatically with another fire at Milford. It began in the hotel kitchen and before being brought under control had destroyed the centre of the building. I went in to Milford two days after the fire and what a shambles it was. With the heart of the hotel gutted it made a spectacle exceeding in desolation that of the 1950 fire.

An evening to honour the firefighters was presided over by Mr Gfeller. On his way into Milford to begin the new season, he had spent the night at Te Anau. Telling of his reaction to the news of the fire, he said he was awakened early, but still half in dreamland, acknowledged the tidings by saying "Good! good!" Another attempt by the disturber of his peace brought "Fine, that's fine!" The third attempt was a shouted "The Milford Hotel is BURNED DOWN!"

"What! what!" he yelled in reply and was halfway along the corridor before he realised he had better get some clothes on. As he continued in this expansive mood, his audience began to think the fire was almost worthwhile in providing a spark that could touch off such an entertaining oration. In lauding the prowess of the firefighters, he said he had known many hotels razed by fire and in every instance when the fire started in the kitchen, the hotel was doomed. Milford was the exception and the reason undoubtedly was the competence and courage of the men they were honouring.

For me the fire was not a dead loss for I salvaged a quantity of good timber and got it over to Sandfly.

With commendable zeal, no time was lost in rebuilding and for the coming season it was Business as Usual at Milford.

The time now semed right to try again to get supplies taken to Doughboy by mechanical means instead of by packhorse. Some years before it had been decided to put in the necessary work during the off-season, but for some reason the matter had been left. To get things moving, I offered to take in a tractor to assist in the necessary road improvements and demonstrate the value of the service it could give. This offer was accepted and before the end of the season it was delivered to Sandfly Point. My son Jack and son-in-law Jack Caldwell bought the Ferguson tractor for me and brought it in. We had some anxious moments getting it off the launch and when it moved under its own power the horses eyed it with critical interest. Jack and Dorothy remained for a few days, Jack working with me putting in some small bridges to take the tractor over, and Dorothy presiding over the pots and pans.

To anyone knowing the Track the advantages of mechanical transport over packhorses were obvious. The horses were kept in a very limited area where they could get no grass and in wet weather trampers had to wade through a slush of mud and manure churned up by the restless hooves. Barbed wire fences and gates, while adding nothing to the scenic attractions, were a nuisance to all who passed through, and visitors taking a trip over on the launch saw nothing at the Point to encourage them to make a more extended acquaintance with the Track, while those saying farewell to it would have their impressions coloured by their last view of it. To horse-lovers the packhorses were of sufficient attraction to excuse anything undesirable that went with them, but not all trampers belong to that category.

Teddy, a hack, too light for heavy packing, was usually left behind and idle time gave him opportunity to think up mischief. When a tramper came along Teddy would fill the gap between the loading ramp and trolly and when the tramper proceeded to find a way round the other side he promptly dodged round to seal that off too. This was disconcerting to some trampers who couldn't see that there was no malice intended but only a demand for some titbit they might be good enough to donate. Teddy became addicted to sweets and when he found a home shortly after on a farm the youngsters shared theirs with him. On one occasion his new owner, while riding on the road, put his hand in his pocket for a sweet. Hearing a rustle of paper the brisk trot came to a sudden stop, round came the head, in popped the lolly and off he went again.

Dispensing with the horses and a packer was a sound economic proposition. Barney Lang had found a good landing for a dinghy near the mouth of the Cleddau River, and he now brought over the daily stores. Any bulk shipments would still be brought by launch, and other items could be delivered when it went over to meet a party. One man, it was assumed, could then without assistance convey the stores from the hotel to Boatshed. This set-up would, I thought, eliminate much friction which periodically arose when stores, expected to reach Quintin, failed to make their appearance. The many stages and handlings multiplied chances of non-delivery. The question was whether they had come over from Milford, been left at Sandfly, Doughboy or Boatshed. Packers' opinions on priorities did not always correspond with those of the Quintin manager and some items would be set aside temporarily, then forgotten.

I discovered one at Boatshed. This was a map of Fiordland. I had written to the Shell people for it, explaining the value it would be to trampers passing through Quintin. After some time, getting no map and no acknowledgment of my letter, I concluded I had presumed too much on their generosity and thought no more about it. I had other thoughts when I found that they had sent it nicely framed under glass and well-packed. But it had got wet in transit and by now was a mouldy ruin. I wrote again to Shell, explaining what had happened and promptly this time received a new map.

It is not surprising there were a few delays between Milford and Quintin. It might be an innocent misunderstanding that precipitated a dialogue, as happened between Norman and John. The article in dispute had not made the grade to Quintin and enquiries indicated that it was nowhere on the Track. "It must be," came a further declaration from Milford, "I saw it put on the launch." After a further inquisition, involving all possible carriers, the argument was again thrown back at Milford. The solution came at last when they found one was speaking of cake, the other of coke.

During this season, the last before the elimination of the packing stage between Sandfly and Boatshed, it seemed this mischievous sprite, if sprite it was, was determined to have her last fling. In the early part of the season I was mostly down at the Sandfly end of the track, but not far enough away to be out of earshot of the rumblings from Quintin. Very soon I was reminded by the Quintin manager quite forcibly of my duty as track foreman to keep supplies moving up the Track. My soft answer didn't seem to convince nor turn away wrath, and I was sure of it when after poking round at Sandfly a day or two later the manager of Milford remarked, "I see no stores here."

"No," I said, "we don't allow anything to accumulate here."

Now for the first time Te Anau was cited as possibly harbouring the elusive supplies.

One evening Mr Marshall, chairman of the Tourist Hotels Corporation, along with some members and Mr Gfeller met for a general discussion to which I was invited. I outlined the proposal to mechanise the Sandfly-Doughboy packing stage, at the same time giving my assurance that with a four-man team (preferably six) going in early, the road would be open for the beginning of the season. They gave me every encouragement by expressions of approval of the scheme and the belief that I would successfully carry it out. After the tramping season closed I worked on till the end of May, being joined by my son Arthur for the last two or three weeks.

The week before we went out we felt an earthquake, the heaviest I have ever experienced. This was during the night, and after it had woken me up I let it rattle away till it subsided before I got up. Arthur was in another hut so I went along to see what he thought of the performance. Outside the hut I could hear the movement of rocks on the mountain tops but nothing near me. At almost every hour of the day and night for the next week there were following quakes, some preceded by a rumble in the direction of the head of the Arthur Valley. One day, walking up the Track I heard the familiar sound and pausing to see if it might be a plane on a scenic flight, I noticed the crown of a tree fern on the lower side of the track quivering. The seat of the earthquake was fifty miles out at sea. It registered force four at Invercargill and seven at Milford and we were probably the nearest people to its source.

Earthquakes are comparatively common in Fiordland and there is always the possibility of an outsize one occurring as it has done in the past. Lake Ada was evidently brought into being by an earthquake precipitating the mountainsides across the Arthur Valley and damming the river back to a distance of eight miles. More than half of that distance has been reclaimed by silt and subsequent slips. Left behind during this process are fragments of the original lake seen in various lagoons. Lake Brown, the largest of these, nestles at the foot of the cliffs on the side of the Wick Mountains.

In 1962 a team from Victoria University, Wellington, made a survey of the lake to determine its age and gain any relevant data. I asked them to let me know the result of their findings, which they later sent me. Carbon dating from samples of submerged tree stumps of silver beech placed the age of the lake at 924 years. Early soundings had registered a depth of seventy feet, but fifty was the deepest they could find. This beautiful lake is now filling comparatively rapidly in the gap between Shoulder Hill and Mt Sheerdown. Here the three main streams, Arthur, Joe's, and Giant's Gate converge. Giant's Gate Delta, spreading its fingers far out into the lake will, in a short time geologically speaking, be joined by the advancing sandbanks from the Arthur River. In 1950 there was open lake up to Red Hut (now gone) beyond the rock bluff of Shoulder Hill, but now the lake proper begins a quarter of a mile distant. We grieve to see these beautiful lakes filling up, the glaciers shrinking and both the effect of introduced pests on bird life and vegetation, but each generation is hardly aware of change and can enjoy in the same measure as their forebears the present glories revealed to them.

Accompanied by Zygmunt Kepka I went in early in the 1960-61 season from Glade House and we went up to Pompolona on 10 September. Rain fell lightly while we were on the way, but increased to a downpour during the night, and for two days let up only for a brief hour or so. During our first night at Pompolona, avalanches began to thunder as they crashed down into the valley. It did not seem possible they could keep coming down day and night, hour by hour, without losing their frequency and intensity. The steady drumming of the rain on the roof, subdued only by the greater crescendo of the avalanches, filled our waking hours and merged with our slumbers. Following each avalanche at the head of the creek, the blast, almost as quick as the sound, stirred the trees round our dwelling. On two occasions snow accompanied the blast and bespattered the hut.

On the morning of the third day we were able to move on. The creek at Pompolona, which was bare of snow when we arrived, was now filled and the avalanche extended across the river, which, however, had kept its channel open. Beyond Pompolona we passed over avalanches varying in depth up to twenty feet or more. As a result of the heavy rain, snow on the Pass was patchy and did not hold us up much.

We found Quintin in very good shape. Zyg, without any expectation of getting an answer, gave the phone a casual ring. I don't know who was the most surprised, he or Brian Vivien who was whitebaiting at Sandfly, when he heard the phone as he was passing the hut, and answered it. I thought Zyg was having me on by pretending there was someone on the line. We were glad to hear Brian and have his assurance we would get over with him to Milford.

Zyg went out but I remained to get on with the work. Early in October I was joined by Tom Wilson, who had been a guide at Waitomo.

As there was a possibility of a jetboat going on to Lake Ada, I thought I would take a look at the river above Boatshed to see how far it would be practicable to take the stores. Tom went on up the Track, while I took my plywood dinghy up to a distance of a mile beyond Diamond Creek. I didn't know then that I wasn't the first to take a dinghy up there. William Quill knew all about that part of the river, as I found out later.

Beyond the rapids at Diamond Creek there was a beautiful quiet stretch of water and although trout are not found far beyond this they are as numerous here as anywhere lower down. At a bend above this placid reach, the river cuts into the bank, bringing down trees which fill the river from bank to bank.

As I could go no farther with the boat, I pulled it up on the bank and made my way up the river, coming on to the Track at the site of the old Slip Camp. I followed Tom up the Track and took a stroll up the Pass Track to see what timber had come down on it since Zyg and I had come over. We spent the night at Quintin and at three o'clock in the morning I heard the first drops of rain on the iron roof. Waking Tom I told him I was off down the Track to make sure of the boat in case the rain became heavier and the river rose. Dawn was just breaking when I reached the boat, as travelling had been slow, particularly on the untracked riverbank. Like William Quill, I found it exciting shooting the rapids, but I could not take them all in this manner, for my plywood job wasn't able to take the knocks it would get from the timber below the rapids, which I could not avoid. The rain did not come to much, nevertheless I was not sorry to have made an early start to get away from what William Quill called that "wicked place". I found that while a jetboat could get up as far as I had gone, it would be

Mt Hart reflected in
Lake Stephen at the
MacKinnon Pass.

ᴇ: The Milford
k in the Clinton
Valley.

ᴛ: Lyndsay Falls.

The Quintin MacKinnon Memorial Cairn on MacKinnon Pass.

ABOVE LEFT: Mt Balloon reflected in L Jeanette.

Triple Falls on the Arthur River.

LEFT: The Sutherland Falls from Maysview the Anderson Track.

of little use as low ground between the landing and the track would be under water at every flood. To take the stores to Diamond Creek where the river touches the track, three-quarters of a mile from Boatshed, would be of little advantage.

Each end of the Milford Track saw unusual activity this season. The packing stage at Glade as well as at Sandfly was being mechanised. The objective at Glade was Six Mile Hut and the road-making was undertaken by the Ministry of Works. Progress was slower than expected, as many such jobs prove in this type of country, but the road was made usable to the four-mile sign. This was a worthwhile step forward in reducing the distance the horses had to cover. The ten-mile stage was tough on the horses, as they had to work in all weather, with loads, on occasion, up to 400 pounds.

Here, where the kiwi, weka and takahe still roamed, it is not surprising that the "horses versus motor" issue was still hotly debated. In all my years on the Track the debate went on with little diminution but none was eloquent enough to convert the other to his point of view. The horse, it is claimed, has a far greater attraction for the tourist than any type of mechanical device. The decline in numbers throughout the country enhances their value here.

From the beginning the walk has been known and gained renown as a track. Turning it into a road destroys the basic elements that constitute the lure of foot travel. Tracks were made before roads. A road gives the impression of settlements and towns. The sight of wheel-marks instead of hoof-marks takes away the impression of isolation from the busy world. A track is the appropriate means of access in opening and preserving nature's unspoilt hinterlands. A road brings a greater risk of despoliation. Preference for the horse and the track, springing mainly from sentiment, is nonetheless a valid and powerful argument.

Those who say the horse has had its day are influenced more by practical and economic factors than by sentiment. They point out that good packhorses are a costly item both in outlay and upkeep. They make a track hard to keep in repair as they keep to the middle, wearing down the crown and allowing the water to gather and scour it out. Material for maintenance cannot economically be packed. The Track when originally formed was six feet wide, very little additional width being required to allow a jeep to get along it. A good example of undamaged original track may be seen near Quintin where the width by no means detracts from its charm.

145

K

A narrow track requires constant trimming in places where growth is rapid. This makes unsightly dead and multilated verges, whereas a wider track to a much greater degree can be left alone to give an appearance of unspoiled natural beauty.

All the fears that the track would be ruined seemed to be realised when the Ministry of Works tore it to pieces along the Clinton and applied rough shingle. But after a time it settled down, and with the application of suitable surfacing material it has been restored to its original condition. Going through the track in March 1968 with Sandy Brown I found the first six miles again in the best walking condition to be found on the whole track.

Many cumbersome pieces of machinery and equipment have been manhandled over miles of the Track because they could not be packed. A concrete mixer was wheeled on a barrow from Glade House to Pompolona, a three-day job. After being landed at Six Mile by tractor and trailer, a six-hundred-gallon tank was carried by four men to Pompolona. At the Milford end the dinghy for Lake Ada took about a week to manhandle from Sandfly to Doughboy. From Boatshed a stove took ten men as many days to drag it to Quintin. These and many similar exploits created much interest and provided many humorous incidents, but these antics are less a joke than plain stupidity when powered conveyance can be employed. The weight of evidence in favour of the motor won the day and for better or for worse, it now is banishing the horse from the Track.

At Sandfly we made our assault on the Track, determined to succeed in getting it through to Doughboy before the tramping season began. I started off with one good man, and although Milford did its best to engage others, the efforts bore no fruit. For one reason and another something intervened between the engagement and the arrival and only two men got as far as the Track. One man, drunk on arrival at Milford, fell out of the bus and broke his arm. To make sure of the next one I went to meet him at Milford and took him straight over to Sandfly. Unfortunately, I had to go up to Quintin and in my absence he went back to Milford for more of his belongings. He also imbibed to excess, ran foul of the Milford authorities and, having put in only one day on the Track, was gone when I returned. Another man who had no high regard for the pick and shovel one afternoon suddenly resigned, saying there were now machines to do that work. It was idle to remind him we were preparing the Track for those very machines, so he packed up and off he went.

I was left now with only one, Tony Ellis. We were about to start the tough job of bypassing the steep, twisted Little Annie, so I said to Tony we would have to bypass this bypass or we would never get through to Doughboy in time. As it was, we broke through the last chain of the tough, rocky little rise at Doughboy only the day before the horses and stores came over from Milford. This was on 18 November, only a fortnight before the opening of the Track. The surface was exceedingly rough in places and for transport we used a sledge. I had expected that with a full team I would have been able to have two men on the follow-up job of surfacing and putting in culverts and watertables. In spite of this, we were really elated in accomplishing what we did.

As we expected, Little Annie gave us no end of trouble, but to compensate Camp Oven Creek gave us none. This creek all along was my only real concern. It had a steel bridge over it, but this, although strong enough, was too narrow to take the tractor. The season before I had got Ray Wilson, Ministry of Works engineer, and others to have a look at it and pass an opinion on the feasibility of making use of it. The obvious thing to do was to split it and move one side over, which was done, but not until six years later when Mervyn Brown made a first-class job of it.

As time was passing with no sign of official approval for the work, I asked for a ton of cement to make a concrete right-of-way across the creek. What appeared a huge job we did in one day, finishing at two o'clock in the afternoon. We made a dry mix in the barrow, wheeled it to the spot, filled a sack right where it was wanted, eased it down into place and flattened it out. We had no certainty our track would stand a flood and could only wait and see. We were afraid, too, that high water would frequently hold up passage through with the tractor. Our fears on both scores proved groundless, for not once was the tractor held up that season and, only at the Sandfly end, a bag or two occasionally shifted.

The mountain of non-perishable stores landed at Sandfly was dealt with expeditiously by Tony and Barney and it says a lot for their industry that these goods were all deposited at Boatshed in the matter of a few days. To make this possible, Barney made two or three trips a day up the lake. Cess Star, confronted with this stack of goods to pack to Quintin, likewise made the most of his time and by early January had cleared the last remaining item.

I had other things to attend to at Quintin and Tony, as soon as he had shifted the stores to Doughboy, set to work on the by-pass, and had it almost completed when the axe fell and he had to go. I had intended leaving him there for the season. He would then have had the road in good enough condition for a trailer. This now had to be postponed.

I much regretted Tony's departure. His interest was in the job rather than the clock and the pay packet. Without his support I could not have accomplished in the time at my disposal the formidable task I had undertaken.

I finished off the bypass, allowing Barney to speed up his service. He was now shifting the stores from Milford to Boatshed without assistance and arriving between 10.30 and 11 o'clock. He frequently had the boat unloaded in time to ferry the trampers across the river. This performance fully justified the change over from horses to tractor and at Sandfly the unsightly fences, gates and mud disappeared to allow the place to take on an appearance more befitting the end of the World-Famous Walk.

I had often heard the desire expressed by trampers to see the region that lay beyond the top of the Sutherland Falls. To make this possible I inspected the spur of Mt Elliot facing the falls, the most likely spot for a good viewpoint. I first studied the spur from MacKinnon Pass, and with my eye followed a likely route starting from the Pass Track a mile from Quintin. Going from there straight up through the bush to the lighter growth of ribbonwood, then turning abruptly to the left to follow a southerly direction, a walker would reach the end of the ridge. Another abrupt turn, this time to the right, leads through the steep tussocky slopes, eventually to gain the higher bare ridge.

I went over this route and found it tough enough in two or three places but not dangerous, and quite within the capabilities of the fit members of a party. On my return I went down through the bush on the most direct line I could find to Quintin, but found it too steep to make use of in ordinary circumstances. Uplifted high on the spur, it narrowed to a mere wall between the deep-cut Roaring Creek and the deeper Arthur Valley, with a magnificent view of Sutherland Falls and Lake Quill; this I was sure would satisfy the most fastidious budding climber. I looked forward to opening up this feature early in the next season.

16

FOREMAN TURNS GUIDE

BEFORE THE NEXT SEASON opened I received a letter from Milford Hotel manager saying that at a meeting of the Board it had been decided to put a younger man in my place and that Cess Star was now appointed Track Foreman. This same letter informed me that if I didn't wish to sever my connection with the Tourist Hotel Corporation I could guide around Quintin.

After the first mixed feelings I chose to stay. There were still so many things to be done in which I was interested that I felt I would like to put in another year or two at least. My years no doubt warranted superannuation but I didn't feel them weighing on me. The track is a healthy place, and, while I lost weight during the season, the strenuous life builds up strength and energy. Good meals, regular hours, the best exercise in the world, walking, perfectly pure water from the mountain streams to replace the loss by profuse sweating; these promote health and kept me young.

My relations with the new foreman were not in the slightest degree affected by the reversal of our status.

The first job I turned my hand to was the blazing of a track up the spur of Mt Elliot. This done, two days' cutting through the bush, fern and ribbonwood beyond it made a track that could be followed without difficulty by the more active tramper. On the tussock slopes I marked the route with light poles of ribbonwood. With the bark stripped off they showed up well enough to keep walkers on the right track.

Shortly after the tramping season opened, I took one young Aussie up the track to try it out. He was George Wisely, from Victoria. He enjoyed the adventure and from his reactions I felt sure many more would be pleased to follow. The next I guided up was also an Australian, a young lady, Natalie Evers. This time I thought I would try out a reasonable-looking short cut but it wasn't as good as it looked, and for safety I used the rope in making a retreat. I think my charge was inwardly pleased at this diversion, her first modest introduction to mountaineering.

After about two hours' travel from Quintin the first glimpse of Lake Quill can be seen. There is a difference in its colour from one day to another. It might be light glacier green, deep blue, purple, black or any of the shades in between with sometimes dual colours. At 4,000 feet there is a little tarn I named Lake Natalie after the visit of the first lady to this spot. From the edge of the ridge near the tarn you can take a photo of Quintin, Sutherland Falls and Lake Quill all in one shot.

I took my true line level up with me and from known heights, MacKinnon Pass 3,400 feet (at the Cairn), top of Sutherland Falls, 3,084 feet, Mt Pillans 5,100 feet, marked the altitude.

On this narrow spur I experience a great uplifted feeling, almost of fear, as some describe it. On the floor of the Arthur Valley so far below, I look down on the little clearing and dot of Quintin, on every turn and twist of the river and creeks, and on the sightseeing plane, floating like a leaf on a smooth flowing current in a deep ravine. The beautiful Green Valley is spread at my feet and Dumpling Hill in its midst, changed at this altitude from its conical form to the flat empty platter from which the dumpling could have been served. From the hump above Lake Natalie the great rifts of Diamond Creek and Mackay Creek coming into the Arthur from the west forcibly meet my eye. In the opposite direction the red dot of Crows' Nest looks up from the depths of Roaring Creek while the track from it is visible to the top of the Pass, which at its lower altitude is spread and smoothed out in its every detail.

When the daily parties gave place to three a week with the full day at Quintin, I would take up groups of about six or eight on an average count. Thirteen was the most taken in one party. Nor did that sinister number cause any misgivings or spoil our day. We generally left Quintin about nine in the morning. I would take the lead and keep the pace down on the steep grade of the first mile up the Pass track. With a short spell at the turn-off, all were in form to attack the stiffer climb ahead. To help heave the old frame up through the bush, I cut away no more than was absolutely necessary, and grips for either hand were generally within reach where they were needed. As progress conformed to the speed of the slowest member of the party, we usually had frequent stops and spells, but with these reduced to the minimum in time and in number, a good performance was still possible.

The usual moaning would be heard when we reached seemingly endless steep tussocky slopes. This, of course, I never took too seriously but there are always some who, partly for their own sake and partly for the sake of others, will say, "Go on, leave us here till you come back." But very few actually do accept this as their Waterloo. After a rest the clear crisp air will get them up on to their feet again and they struggle along after the others. There was a girl whose leg muscles got so sore she declared she could go on no farther, but by this time she also had an equally demanding thirst and could only be satisfied by going on to where there was water. The thirst, unlike the legs, didn't improve with a spell and at each of the increasingly frequent stops, the argument between the thirst and the legs was renewed. I assured her that the little tarn (Lake Andrew) was only a little distance ahead, and when we reached this longed-for dew pond, she flattened out beside it and cured at least one of her complaints. And on the way down, her legs worried her not the slightest.

On these trips I would take up just enough food to make a scanty lunch, and boil the thermette at Lake Natalie.

The only fuel there was was the dead stems of the snowgrass, but it did the job quite well. I left the cups in the tarn so that the keas would not play with them and break them, and all I had to carry up was the thermette and rations. While I was boiling up, the cameras were busy at the edge of the ridge getting a photo of Lake Quill, Sutherland Falls and Quintin. The more active members would scale the hump, another 1,000 feet, not far above which the true line levelled off with the top of Mt Pillans.

After our snack I would round up the party and keep them together as it is easy to be led off from the right course on the way down. We only did this trip when we were sure of fine weather, and a sunny day made the snowgrass as slippery as ice to glissade on. Sliding down the slopes at high speed raised great hilarity, and well repaid the struggle going up. By getting back to Quintin at three o'clock we had time for a cup of tea before setting off up to the Sutherland Falls. From there I would bring them back over Christie Falls bridge and down the other side of the river where the Giant's Castle with its mysterious twilight underground passages, caverns and waterfalls made a striking contrast to the sunshine and heights from which they had so lately descended.

Those putting in the day at Quintin would go round Anderson Track and get a full-length photo of the Sutherland Falls, but the Elliot party got theirs plus Lake Quill, and, having reached the foot of the falls and gone through Giant's Castle, they felt they were missing very little the others had enjoyed.

The extra day at Quintin, allowing the trampers to do justice to the additional side attractions, proved a most popular innovation. After a two-day hike many need an easy day and it is up to them whether they make a lazy day of it or not. On the second day the climb over the Pass can be made more leisurely when a visit to the Sutherland Falls can be postponed till the following day. In favourable weather the day on the Pass is all too short. Here the botanist is in clover, and so is the photographer. Here the most casual cannot escape an elevation of spirit on this uplifted grandstand, displaying a grand sweep of mountain peaks and yawning canyons. But when the weather is bad with poor visibility many take the opportunity to return from Quintin the following day.

When walkers are limited to three days on the Track, many miss the most notable feature, the Sutherland Falls, as they are too tired to make the effort of another mile and a quarter at the close of a long hard day. Those who do make the effort see it at the poorest viewing time of the day, the late afternoon, when the sun no longer gives sparkling life to the descending waters, nor are they in the mood fully to appreciate the magnificence of this display. On the other hand, the extra day enables the tramper to view and photograph the fall in all its glory with a magnificent rainbow added as good measure, when the sun is shining.

One man who had gone through the Track some years before, told me he was mystified why the extra day at Quintin was included when he booked for his second trip. There was nothing to see, he thought, but the Sutherland Falls and an additional day was not needed for that. After he had put in a full day at Quintin he was in no doubt about its value. With the proven advantage of the four-day programme, this could very well be made the pattern for every party throughout the season. It would mean doubling up the accommodation at Quintin, but not all the amenities or the staff. Besides providing a more popular service, it would be financially profitable. Very definite and divergent views are expressed by those who on the one hand favour full exploitation of the Track's potentialities, and on the other by those who would concentrate on the main track and keep to modest proportions the number going through. With some reason the latter believe that the upgrading of the main track needs the staff's full attention. They say a better walking surface would add more to the enjoyment of the average tramper than additional new features. The size of the parties at present, forty, is ideal. Larger ones would destroy the spirit of "doing this thing together" which a small party engenders.

Those with expansionist ideas say that with growing competitive attractions, the Milford Track cannot stay as it is and in addition to an improvement of the main track, other avenues of interest to the tramper should not be neglected. To make financial ends meet the Milford Track, like any business venture, is compelled to meet inexorable pressure from rising costs.

It has been stated that with daily parties forty strong, saturation point has been reached and from a financial point of view the Track is doomed. This we know is absurd. Glade House could be extended to accommodate many besides the track walkers who would like to spend a few days making acquaintance with the glorious Clinton River and its superb fishing. Quintin could open its doors to pilgrims from Milford and regain its role as host to excursionists and others as it did seventy years ago.

While these issues are considered and at times hotly debated by management and staff, the tourists themselves have ideas which after all should be treated with respect. The first requirement, stated by Sir Thomas McDonald upon his return from the post of High Commissioner in London, was a friendly manner in all contacts with tourists, not an artificial veneer, but a genuine interest in their welfare. Tourists are individuals and as far as possible their separate wishes should be gratified. Of course there is a definite limit beyond which an endeavour to please everybody would result in pleasing nobody.

A middle-aged lady lectured me on the advantages of keeping the Track comparatively rough. "If you make it too easy," she said, "you will have all the vandals and riff-raff coming through and spoiling it for others." Her last words as she left Quintin were, "Now remember what I've told you. Don't make the Track any easier."

Some speedy individuals are concerned with nothing but getting from one point of the Track to another in the shortest possible time. Others are not concerned enough about the passage of time while they make the most of what is to be seen by the way. Some are insatiable, and having filled the regular programme still ask what more we have to offer.

One such enterprising tramper, anxious to go back from Quintin to the MacKinnon Pass to capture what was denied her by the unfavourable weather the day before, prudently desisted because of aches and pains which she thought would prove too great a hindrance to herself and others in the party. To compensate I provided a full morning's activity taking the stay-at-homes round Anderson Track to the Sutherland Falls and returning via Giant's Castle. Once she warmed up, this lady lost every trace of stress and strain and frequently bewailed the loss of opportunity to see the Pass again. I said nothing but told her not to dawdle too long over lunch. With a half-day instead of a full day free to visit the Pass it hadn't occurred to her that it was possible.

I didn't want to raise her hopes too much in case she found the going too heavy, so merely suggested we go back up and meet the others coming down. Still going strong she met her husband coming down the side of the Pass. He turned back with her to the Pass while I put in time until they returned at work on the Track. I then took them a short cut down the emergency track, and showed them the Moraine Creek waterfalls. As he had not been up to the Sutherland Falls, her husband made the trip in the morning and she accompanied him. Beginning with such poor prospects, she finished up doing more than any had previously done and left Quintin a very satisfied tramper.

Many a time when I have been at Sandfly as a party arrived I would ask them which feature or section of the Track they enjoyed most. Their answers, though varied, were generally consistent in favouring the place where genuine interest was taken in them and friendly hospitality shown, whether on the Track or at the lodges. Trampers are very quick to detect any feeling of restraint towards them. The scenery is not enough. Cool treatment will give the scenery a bleak look, and on the other hand, if the contacts with staff are all they should be you may depend upon it that the scenery will be lovely.

Most of the trampers pass only once through the Track. Some have planned and waited long before being able to realise their desire. Surely it is nothing short of a tragedy that such people should be treated casually and left with the impression that the Track was not nearly so enjoyable as they expected. Other resorts that have nothing like the wealth of scenery to display make the utmost of their opportunity to entertain and welcome their patrons, and in so doing make inroads on their more favoured competitors. Strange to say, this most vital quality appears to carry little weight in appointments to the staff. One may sum up briefly thus: there are two classes of people on the staff of this, or any other resort. There are those who are there to serve the interests of the tourist and the others to serve their own interests.

The 1961-62 season started well but did not carry on long in that manner. There were changes in staff that threw the works out of joint. Cess Star left shortly after coming in and Tom Milburn, who had been Pass Guide, took his place. This was before the tramping season started. Carpenters were making alterations to the building and I, the only one left, found a job packing timber for them. When more men came, I carried on packing while they manhandled the heavy units being installed for the hot water system and for cooking. The old heater installed in 1932, which had given excellent service, was replaced by a drip-feed diesel unit. Another to serve the staff ablution section was installed at the kitchen, and a stove, diesel-fired, installed for cooking.

During this season I put in some work on the Moraine Creek track, making it much more negotiable. Two of my grandsons were employed on the track and near the end of the season I got their help to erect a suspension bridge over Roaring Creek.

I had assembled the component parts the season before and I found it gruelling work. I designed the bridge to involve as little carrying as possible, chain mesh, fencing wire and the two main ropes five-eighths of an inch and each forty-four yards in length. The day I carried up most of the material from Quintin was exceedingly hot. At noon I went along to Crows' Nest to boil the billy and, as every stitch I had on was saturated with perspiration, I stripped them all off, spread them on the bushes and while the sun was at work, wore a blanket. In only a matter of minutes the blazing sun had them completely dry, so on they went again and I went back to my carrying.

We put up the bridge in a week. It measured 100 feet. There was now a safe way down from Crows' Nest.

Before I put the bridge over Moraine Creek a party, one rainy day, were brought down in two lots. The first-comers were taken down and crossed Moraine Creek all right, but the increasing rain put Roaring Creek up so high they were caught between them, for by this time Moraine was also too high. The second party were not able to cross and were taken down the emergency track to Quintin. The first party had to put in a miserable night at Crows' Nest, but at least they had a roof over them, and were able to keep a fire of sorts going. They finished their journey in time for breakfast at Quintin in the morning.

Some enquiry was made by one of the interested airlines about providing an airstrip at Quintin. The hotel manager, Mr Alexander, favourably disposed to the project, was pleased to accept the offer of my son Jack to make a rough preliminary survey. He did so and found the project a simpler one than anticipated. The survey maps were left at Milford as a guide for the later making of the landing strip.

Later on in the season Zygmunt Kepka was appointed Track Foreman and that same winter it was decided to open up the way between Boatshed and Quintin for wheels to replace horses. The smouldering fires of the old argument burst again into flame, and a compromise was made that a horse-drawn instead of a motor-driven vehicle would be employed. My increasing years apparently didn't count any longer for I was put in charge of the work party.

17

A WINTER ASSIGNMENT

THE WINTER OF 1963 was the only one I worked right through on the Track. With me were Tony Donne, Glyn De Torres and my grandson, William Caldwell. These men were workers and first-class to get along with, both on and off the job. Later on, Graham Hill took the place of my grandson when he had to go into military camp.

We settled in at Boatshed when the tramping season closed in April, and towards the end of the month started to work our way up the Track.

I set up my rain gauge and from 15 April until the same date the next year it recorded 274 inches. Forty-seven inches were recorded in May, and that put a damper on our work right in its early stages. Although there is usually less rain in the winter than in other seasons, work is not then so easily done. The few hours of sunshine leave a dampness in the air when two or three degrees of frost feel like twenty. A wet winter such as this one takes all the profit and most of the pleasure from the work. An hour and a half of sunshine was all we got at mid-winter. The long nights were brightened by Tilley lamps, while the damp and cold were kept partially at bay with kerosene heaters and a coal range.

We took turns at going down to Milford for mail and perishable supplies. Time spent this way, and lost by wet weather, could not be made up as in summer with its long daylight hours, but the progress we made was quite good.

When the horses were taken out for the winter, we kept one, big grey Pepper. He was known as a good reliable collar horse. We soon found how good he was. We used him mainly to haul bridge timber from the bush to the big creeks at Racecourse Flat. Pepper must have been broken in by a Maori because he would not settle down to business until he had performed his war-dance. After these preliminaries he was off like a shot. It was all or nothing with him and woe betide the man who was leading him if he fell by the wayside. One day, while I was getting him started (it was a sword dance this time) he clapped his big foot on mine. The surface was uneven and I was thrown to the ground. He kept that foot on mine for what seemed an age while he performed with the other three. Nothing is so bad that it mightn't be worse, for he could have chosen that moment to dart off and pull the load over me. A good bush horse is worked without reins, directed merely by word of command, but Pepper was not that kind of horse. The safest way I found was to use a long rein; one was enough to pull him up as he was well enclosed by the Track.

I had trouble though with two or three logs that were longer than the rein, and that was when it came to my turn for the sword dance. It took good judgment to tell where the log was going to be and when. The Track gave little room for manoeuvre and less time to look before the leap. As an exercise for an aspiring Olympic athlete I know of none better. I wouldn't claim it would turn out the finished article, but following a horse at speed, handicapped by the side-stepping over this unpredictable hurdle, would perhaps serve to weed out some of the aspirants in the early stages.

One other time, when Pepper had finished his display and shot off the mark, I let the spare length of rein run through my hand, relying on the knot at the end to act as clutch. But the knot this time was gone and so was the horse. He was headed in the direction of Quintin and would soon be there if he kept up the pace he started. I followed leisurely and found him a quarter of a mile away where the stringer he hauled had fouled the bank of a creek at a bend in the Track. We had intended using him in the jogger to go to and from work when we reached a mile or two from Boatshed, and we expected to find and pick up surfacing gravel on our way and cart the lighter bridge timbers. We did not yoke him up very often after we came to know him and each time we unyoked him we heaved a thankful sigh of relief that we'd had no disaster. The number of times he went into reverse, every time backing into the bank instead of into the gully, was the kind of luck we didn't dare push too far.

In August we reached a quarter of a mile from the halfway sign which, with the half-mile opened at the Quintin end, added up to more than half the distance to our objective. We estimated that continuing as we were doing through September, October and

November, we would come near Gentle Annie, leaving only that formidable obstacle for our final efforts.

A halt was now called, however, and the project shelved. This decision I found very frustrating, but it cheered the advocates of the *status quo*. Whether or not they were conscious of it, they were fighting a losing battle, a rearguard action against change. In spite of all they or I could say or do, the day of the packhorse on the track was over.

My preference was for a jeep but they compromised with a horse-drawn vehicle. This all-steel job was declared too heavy for a horse, although I could push it around much more easily than the old-fashioned dray. It was impossible to make a road up Gentle Annie or if we did, they said, a horse couldn't get there with a load. This I knew to be all hooey. The half-ton load in the dray, steel-shod, would in comparison hardly be felt on a rubber-tyred jogger. In the old days on the farm, five and a half miles from the rail, we made two trips a day with waggon and dray. Three tons was a normal load for four horses in the waggon, and we had hills as steep, though not so long, as Gentle Annie. The distance between Boatshed and Quintin being the same, this would also allow two trips if necessary. One horse, then, shifting a minimum of one ton a day, would equal the performance of nine packhorses with 250-pound loads, for they would make only one trip a day. Six horses were in use at the time. The wear and tear on the track of six instead of one is surely obvious. Moreover, there would be only half the time taken in carting and the time thus saved could be put in on track improvement. Packs could be carried for the trampers and when there was nothing else to cart, gravel for track maintenance could be loaded at Roaring Creek.

Had this job been carried to completion, a well-surfaced track would, before long, have been built up. The costly transport by plane and helicopter could have been avoided. The horses have gone, and we have still the rough track with no effective means of upgrading it. The trampers still carry their packs and when the skies are grey Quintin is reduced to an erratic instead of a regular service.

During the winter Zyg Kepka, now Track Foreman, and Dave White were engaged in improving the Sandfly-Doughboy track, taking off some corners which might prove awkward for the transport of the jetboat which was promised for Lake Ada. The jet finally arrived and, after some preliminary trial runs, settled down to efficient regular service skippered by Ron Cox.

I put in the season following the winter job on track work and guiding at Quintin. At the end of the season, as I thought it was time to quit, Mr Bremner, the manager at Milford, paid me my last cheque. But my continued interest in the Track and its history drew me back. Making myself useful here and there I put in the next two seasons.

As my years on the Track lengthened, my opportunities of gathering historical data increased. Many track walkers have knowledge of, or are in touch with someone previously connected with the Track, who may have valuable information. From such I have added to my store of track knowledge. Many after their first visit find their interest in track history whetted to the extent that upon a return they bring more records of the past with them. Many would be on the lookout for me and it is a great pleasure to meet earlier trampers or receive a message from them. One such (an American) greeted me on the Pass with a message from Sandy Brown. Thanking him, I quoted, "How beautiful upon the mountains are the feet of him that bringeth good tidings."

"Sounds like Shakespeare or something," was his observation.

During this period a long needed rest-room was erected at Sandfly and a suspension bridge put up over the Poseidon Creek overflow.

Shamus Coreen followed Glyn De Torres as Track Foreman and he in turn was followed by Mick Arthur.

In addition to the new tractor shed and storeroom at Sandfly, Mick made substantial improvements at Boatshed and erected a bridge over Moraine Creek.

On the Te Anau side of the Track changes in track staff were not so frequent. Ray Willet's last season as Track Foreman was 1961-62. He and his wife Helen then managed Pompolona during the next season before making their farewell to the Track. In every department of track management and guiding he followed worthily in the footsteps of the succession of outstanding men of the Clinton Valley, from Quintin MacKinnon, the first, to Dan Greaney, Ray's immediate predecessor. Ray O'Brien, for years Ray Willet's right-hand man, now took his place and carried on the work with equal distinction and success.

This gum tree, believed planted by Snodgrass in 1890, was removed in 1965.

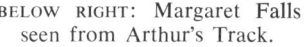

RIGHT: Six Mile Inn.

BELOW RIGHT: Margaret Falls seen from Arthur's Track.

BELOW: Veil Falls on Arthur's Track.

ABOVE: Jack Skinner and party. Bill and Joy Hewitt, host and hostess at Quintin.

RIGHT: Packhorses at Quintin.

BELOW: Mt Elliot, Jervois Glacier, Mt Wilmot, and Lake Ella.

One day early in December a track party arrived at Quintin. In the evening after dinner I went into the guest room, and looking for a game of Scrabble I was introduced to an Aussie from Queensland, Dorothy Smith. This lady was no novice at the game and promptly gained a fifty bonus. Other qualities appealed to me even more than her skill at Scrabble. The attraction was mutual and we were married two months later. Attracted as we both are by the lure of the wilds, we could not altogether sever our connection with the Track.

At Sandfly I had attempted to discover the grave of the prisoner who died in 1891, and now with permission from Milford, Dorothy and I camped in the room which originally was the kitchen in the hut serving the track walkers before Hotel Milford came into the picture. Along with the main building, of which it was a part, it was due for removal, so we negotiated with Milford to make use of it to rebuild on the other side of the river, where we could carry on our search for the grave.

The spot we chose to build on was at the head of the cove above the Sandfly Point landing. A good landing place, a nice little knoll, abundance of driftwood for fuel and a clear running stream make it perfect. The Maoris had thought so too, for they have left evidence of their occupation.

Repeated searches for the grave have proved fruitless. Although I have been in touch with those who saw it years ago their directions have not led me to the spot. At one place I discovered a four-by-one sawn timber peg rotted off near the surface of the ground. Thinking it might indicate the site of the grave, I dug all around but could find no sign of disturbed subsoil. There were a few loose stones on the surface that made me hope that they had come from the strata of rubble five feet below the surface.

My digging was not altogether fruitless for it revealed the interesting evidence that the river once emptied into the Sound from a much higher bed than now. On the bank of the river, twenty or thirty feet above tide level a deposit of fine silt lies on a bed of rubble. From this it would appear that considerable change has occurred at Sandfly since the cataclysm which filled in the valley and formed Lake Ada.

L

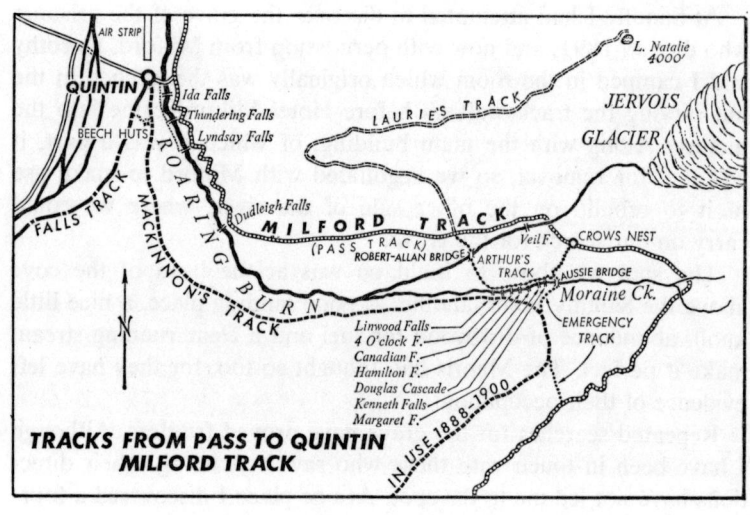

18

STORMY BUT CLEARING

THE END OF THE 1966-67 SEASON was marked by a deluge. Extensive damage was done in the Clinton, but not so much in the Arthur Valley.

The rain started on 20 April 1967 and continued through the next day. On the twenty-second, accompanied by high winds, the rain became much heavier, bringing the Clinton up to high flood level. The twenty-third brought rain and hail, with snow on the tops, followed by more heavy rain on the twenty-fourth and twenty-fifth. At mid-morning on the twenty-fifth avalanches and slips started to roar down between Pompolona and the Eleven and Half-Mile Creek. Again the river reached record high levels. The rain stopped on the afternoon of the twenty-sixth. From the Pass down to Lake Te Anau the havoc was tremendous.

The old Pass Hut had several sheets of iron torn off. The wind had blown the door open, tearing the Dexion steel plate which attached the padlock to the door. The creeks on either side of Pompolona were either scoured out or rocks were piled up at their crossings. On the lower side of Pompolona two chains of track was washed away and a twenty-foot-wide gorge had been cut across the Track.

Every few hundred yards spoke of the destructive power of unbridled floodwaters. At seven and three-quarter miles a new six-foot stretch of heavy corduroy had been shifted forty yards. Along the seven-mile stretch sand had been heaped on to the Track to a depth in places of two feet. A new creek near the Six Mile Inn had washed out a chain of track to a depth of three or four feet. Creeks under some of the bridges had filled up with boulders and the water had washed over them.

At Neale Burn, one and three-quarter miles, there was a hole about seven feet deep and a chain long. At Devil's Elbow, one and a quarter miles, a heap of large trees had been washed up on to the Track and at half a mile the Track had been undermined and

163

collapsed into the river. The wharf at the head of the lake was under three feet of water and driftwood. The *Tawera* entered the Glade Burn overflow to bring in supplies and to take on board Ken Ward, Ministry of Works carpenter, who had been working at Pompolona at the time of the flood. Neither the tractors nor the horses could be used, and all essential items and personal belongings had to be carried out: the horses were brought down unladen. On 8 May the wharf was still under water so the *Tawera* again came to the mouth of Glade Burn overflow to take the Pompolona staff to Te Anau for the winter.

Ray O'Brien with his repair gang came in early in the spring (5 August) to repair the damage to the track and be ready for the opening of the 1967-68 season.

Applying themselves diligently to the task of restoration, they were rewarded by seeing the Track again in good condition. All went well in the new season with nothing to indicate that within the next twelve months a much greater mess would have to be cleaned up.

The year 1968 will probably be remembered by the present generation as the disaster year. In one way or another every part of the country and its coasts was visited by some catastrophe. Flocks and herds snowed in on the high country, floods on the low, wheat crops ruined in the south, terrific storms, shipwreck with heavy loss of life and an earthquake of major dimensions caused one to ask "What next?"

The Milford Track, always vulnerable to nature's fiercer moods, did not escape. Tremendous avalanches filled the ravines and swept the open glades. Slips from the mountainsides, grinding, tearing and pulverising everything on their path, blotted out portions of the Track. In October cyclonic winds passed over these scenes of desolation making confusion worse confounded. Hundreds of trees, scores of them forest giants, crashed down on the Track, challenging men with axe and chain saw to find a way through. This time the Arthur Valley suffered more than the Clinton.

In the autumn we heard that plans were afoot to open to wheeled traffic the packing stage between Six Mile and Pompolona, and also to put in an airstrip at Quintin. We were at Sandfly in May when machinery for the construction of the airstrip was flown in by helicopter. As it droned overhead, carrying all sorts of queer-looking loads, it seemed to herald a new and interesting epoch in track history. Just how interesting and how unexpectedly events were to take shape we could never have guessed.

The airstrip was cleared of timber and a start made on the road to Pompolona, but the heavy winter, the wet spring and finally the big blow in October made the prospect of opening the Track seem in grave doubt. Horses could not be brought in at the normal time, the airstrip was not ready for the planes, nor was the road open to Pompolona. Every effort was made, supplemented by a labour force of thirty boys from the Invercargill Borstal, to bring order out of chaos and finally a date could be set (15 January) for the opening.

A departure was made from the dual control of the Track shared by the hotels at Te Anau and Milford. Te Anau now assumed full responsibility and one supervisor for the whole track was appointed. The appointee was Richard Tubman who had several years on the Track to his credit.

Seldom in track history have such demands been made on the wisdom and experience of a track supervisor. Added to the natural physical difficulties, there was the controversial issue still not fully resolved of whether it was wise to extend the road to Pompolona and go ahead with the airstrip at Quintin. When nature intervened to slow down the work to a standstill, enthusiasm for the project in some quarters diminished in like measure. This apathy actually made a more formidable confrontation than the physical challenge, and in these circumstances Richard showed something of the qualities of his namesake the "Lion Heart". Baulked and frustrated on every hand, he never failed to be the same cheery and bantering guide and host to the track walkers.

Dorothy and I were in at Sandfly before the season opened and, as some extra assistance was needed at Boatshed, we undertook to attend to the work there. Darky Thomas had his headquarters at Boatshed, but as he had occasional fishing parties to convey to the choice spots on Lake Ada and other duties to attend to, a resident caterer would be helpful to provide lunches for the regular track parties. These and the Park Board free walkers had to be ferried across the river. As Dorothy was able to cope with the catering and, at times, ferrying, I found useful occupation on track work. I made the occasional sortie up the track when told from Quintin that some tramper or trampers needed help.

One evening Bill Hewitt rang from Quintin to say a lady tramper was missing. They thought she had missed the turn-off into Quintin and if so could I find her and turn her back? By the time I reached the halfway mark without any sign of her I felt I was on a wild goose chase. Another mile farther on I met Bill who come on down to let me know the wanderer had turned up. As they had suspected, she had taken the track leading to Boatshed, but after a time, realising she must have overshot the mark, she made an about turn and arrived shortly after he had rung me.

This latest example of bypassing Quintin shows that the means employed to prevent it are still not absolutely effective.

One morning I was asked to see how an eighty-seven-year-old gentleman in the party was making out. I found he was not a bit tired, and on a smooth track surface could get along at quite a smart pace, but a limb disability made the walk quite a trial on the rough stretches of the Track. This tramper reminded me of another, a young lady who suffered a strained ligament. Her progress on all but the perfectly level surface was so painfully slow that I persuaded her to accept a pick-a-back and so for the remaining two miles I carried her over the rough spots.

For such as these, and elderly people, a rough track makes difficult and sometimes painful a walk that otherwise should be trouble-free and enjoyable. If the path is smooth they won't care whether you call it a track or a road. If they are able to take their eyes off their feet as they go, they won't notice whether the marks are made by hoofs or wheels.

One day shortly after taking up our duties, Richard Tubman paid Boatshed a visit. Even in this peaceful spot he wasn't going to escape some chafing of the spirit. He came across the river to where I was working and when we returned we found a drum underneath the boat. When we pushed the boat aside the drum followed. We then found it was attached to the stern line. This drum had been the receptacle for refuse and a most appalling odour clung to it. Dorothy applied all the remedies available without much result so took it down to the river to see what the pure waters of the Arthur could do. As convenient a place as any was over the stern of the dinghy attached to a line. Neither when he entered nor left the boat had Richard observed it and now, instead of heaping abuse on the offending and offensive article he was able to appreciate the comic absurdity of straining at the oars to drag it across the riverbed. Coming over he had just thought he wasn't as good with the oars as he used to be.

Richard stayed the night and that evening Darky Thomas, who was writing a letter, complained that there was nothing to write about. Dorothy had spotted a rat somewhere about the premises this day so I started to say: "How can you say that . . ." then hesitated, weighing the effect my words would have before going on, "How can you say that when we have had a visit today from the boss and a rat?"

Richard, having been buffeted by avalanches, gales and slips, was still big enough to laugh as heartily as the others at this jibe.

The weather throughout February was exceedingly hot and dry. Before the season opened we had promised Murray Gunn we would look after his Hollyford Camp at about this time, so we were away during the first half of the month. The weather changed early in March and remained broken, with rain nearly every day till the end of the season. Till near the end temperatures were agreeably mild, but there was a different tale to tell on the Pass, where freezing winds and pelting rain so often plagued the tramper.

During the month I took a run over to Pompolona. Dorothy came as far as Quintin with me, and would have come up to the Pass but rain set in and continued all day. I was interested in seeing the remains of the great avalanche stacked up against the mountain at Roaring Creek. It had receded well above the Track, but I could see it was larger than any I had previously known. The same applied to the one at Pompolona.

The new Pass Hut built at the site of the first one I found bracing itself against the winds at their fiercest, for in this gap between the hump in the middle of the Pass and Mt Balloon the gales tear across at a velocity higher than elsewhere. A Park Board hut was erected during the off-season but before it could be made use of, the big blow in October carried it away. At the same time the Tourist Hotel Corporation hut was wrecked but not shifted from its site. The little old original hut vanished at the same time. Blown down three times in its forty years' service, it held so tenaciously to its foundations that this time it took them away with it. The new hut has two compartments, one for the Park Board trampers, the other for the Tourist Hotel Corporation.

Ric Smith, the Quintin guide, went up before me to the Pass, taking only half the time I took to walk it. He found the matches had vanished and patiently awaited my arrival, hoping I would be able to supply his need. Fortunately I had a box and in a remarkably short space of time had the soup, tea and coffee ready for his wet, perished guests. Richard Tubman guided the party up from Pompolona and I accompanied him on the way down. Once we gained the shelter of the Clinton, conditions were quite pleasant. On the subject of the Track and its maintenance, there was much to discuss so the five miles soon fell behind.

As the next day was fine, I went down to Six Mile with Richard and saw for myself what I had heard described as a stalemate, the attempt to link Six Mile and Pompolona with a road. From my experience of similar work on the Milford side and the performance of the Ministry of Works between Glade and Six Mile, I must say that a very creditable job had been accomplished. Much remained to be done to improve the Track, but there appeared to be no difficulty that couldn't eventually be overcome. Trailer loads of a ton weight have been taken to Pomoplona over the new track, a performance which effectively answers the critics who see only the dark side of the picture.

For about half the distance the new road follows a route near the river where there is good, firm ground. As a bridge had washed away, the tractor and trailer could not take the stores up, so we used the horses. The day was warm as we made our way back to Pompolona, so Richard hung his shirt on one of the pack-saddles. On reaching Pompolona he found it was missing. Instead of the few dammits I expected, Richard treated as a joke the putting of his shirt on a horse and losing it.

On my way back the next day I went down the emergency track, over the "Aussie Bridge" above Margaret Falls and down Arthur's Track.

The big blow in October had brought down so many big trees over the track above Moraine Creek that I had to make my way through the bush for some distance before regaining it. For convenience in servicing the telephone line, this track needs to be reopened. It should also be kept open to use in an emergency. Although Moraine Creek is bridged on the main track the chief danger now is from avalanches coming off the glacier between Elliot and Wilmur Mountains. This is a new danger never experienced until recent times. The Jervois Glacier has now receded, leaving a wider area of bare rock in mid- and late season. Snow during the summer and autumn, which formerly remained attached to the glacier, now much more readily comes away. A ledge on the cliff-face holds a small avalanche but when that can contain no more it glissades off and lands right on the Track. This most frequently happens in the early afternoon when the sun has got round far enough to soften it up and this is the time the trampers reach that danger spot.

On 7 January 1964, after a mere six inches of snow, an avalanche, fortunately a small one and clean, caught a party as it was passing. Dave White and Lloyd Gallagher were with the party. These men were well aware of the danger and Dave, who was close to where it fell, had barely time to warn the trampers to flatten out where they were, before it was upon them. One lady wearing shorts had one side of her thigh and leg cut and bruised. The others got off with a severe fright. Lloyd, who was on the rise on the other side of Moraine Creek about 200 yards away, did not escape its severe blast.

On another occasion when I was at Crows' Nest an avalanche came down as a party was in the vicinity. A great cloud of snow billowed up as it fell on the ledge and as it kept coming I was sure it could contain little more. I made my way in that direction and presently met the first tramper who with great glee told me he had got a superb shot of the avalanche. He and his companions didn't know how near they were to taking their last photo.

At the end of the following season I had spent some little time with Ray O'Brien and went up the Mt Elliot track with him to a height of 5,000 feet. While we were down at Sandfly the Otago Tramping Club went through the Track. They were known as the "Freedom Walkers" as they were out to demonstrate the belief in their right to use the track without seeking permission from the Tourist Hotel Corporation. They encountered heavy rain and found the Track had its hazards. It must have been about this time that a heavy avalanche came down at Moraine Creek after two feet of snow, for when my son Bert, grandson Garth and Ray O'Brien went through in May the snow had melted, leaving the area strewn with rock. To avoid this danger a good, well-graded track could be broken down to a serviceable grade on the route followed by the emergency track. This would shorten the distance and the

169

M

superb Moraine Creek waterfalls could be included in this deviation.

Following the demonstration by the Freedom Walkers the Park Board proceeded to build huts located at suitable intervals on the Track. In the Clinton Valley, four miles from the head of Lake Te Anau, is the Forks Hut; the next is at Lake Mintaro. The third is in the Arthur Valley two and a quarter miles from Quintin, a little below the lower outlet of the creek from Green Valley.

Near the end of the 1968 season, several American fishing parties guided by Ted Tapper made Boatshed their headquarters. They were taken to the fishing grounds both above and below Boatshed in the jetboat. They proved very interesting personalities and what they did not know about fly fishing wasn't worth finding out.

With the roaring season deerstalkers became more active. Looking out from Quintin one day Dane Woods spotted a slight movement in the bushes at the side of the clearing. He could hardly believe his eyes when it materialised into a stag. Quickly he seized his rifle, and signalling the others to lie low he got in a perfect shot that won him a sixteen-pointer. Two stalkers passed through on their way to try their luck up the tributaries of the Arthur River. They must have put in a miserable time with so much rain but they returned triumphantly with a sixteen-pointer secured right on the top of the saddle between Staircase Creek and the Light River. These two men, Messrs Oliver and Severinsen from the North Island, and Cramond, Vaughan and Williams from the United States, joined in a dinner where the atmosphere was well charged with the spirit of the hunting field and the angling stream. Two successful authors in the company, Mike Cramond and Keith Severinsen, each with another book on the way, found much in common to discuss.

Two Canadian girls on the Hotel Te Anau staff stayed a night with us on their way through the Track. Instead of spending a day at Quintin as the other members of the party had done, they had come down expecting to be sped on their way by the jetboat. But it did not come up as the river was high and had they crossed they would have found water over the track at Steep Hill. By delaying their journey till the next day they met the fishing party coming off the launch as they boarded it at Sandfly, and to her surprise one of them recognised Mr Cramond as the father of a friend back in Vancouver.

Stormy But Clearing

We received a surprise too one evening when we heard a halloo from across the river. As it was dark we took a Tilley lamp down to the landing to act as lighthouse. We were trying to guess who the traveller might be so late on the Track, but it wasn't until I reached the other side I found it was George, Dorothy's brother. He had a torch to light his way over the Track which was quite unknown to him. He fared better than two members of the staff, both from Pompolona, neither very familiar with the Track. They had no light and the night was dark. Stumbling, falling and getting off the Track they almost despaired of reaching Boatshed. We were alerted by a cooee and met a very relieved but dishevelled pair.

With the last party of the season Mr Honey made his appearance at Boatshed with four others while the main body of the party put in the day at Quintin. Recalling his previous visit to the Track and his helpfulness at headquarters in Wellington while I was gleaning historical data for my scrap book, I was more than pleased to greet him. I had one of the two beautiful scrap books he had acquired for me and I trust he was not disappointed with the use I had made of it.

With this party, Mr Smythe, assistant manager of Hotel Te Anau, carried the ashes of one, Mrs Margaret Hare of Wanganui, whose love for the Track made the MacKinnon Pass her choice for her resting place.

The forces of nature were tuned for this solemn occasion. The skies bowed their heads in weeping, lowering clouds, while the bleak winds lifted up the ashes to scatter them over the green slopes and ruffled waters of the tarns.

This is not how she had viewed the Pass on her last visit. On that occasion she had gone up from Quintin on a hot midsummer's day. The temperature was 96 degrees at Quintin and 76 at the Pass. She had stayed the night there so that she could see it in the splendour of the rising sun. This was one of the rare occasions when the heat of the day was not entirely dissipated until dawn and she was rewarded with a marvellous calm bright morning. While the valleys were still shrouded in gloom the sun had touched the peaks with its fire.

It may have been at this hour, moved by the serenity and magnificence of the scene, that she resolved that here, where in life she loved to linger, she would make her final resting place.

171

Again the helicopter droned overhead as it had done last autumn, carrying engine blocks, frames and wheels—wheels within wheels "way up in the middle of the air". The equipment this time was for Connelly, who had the contract to complete the airstrip. As Bill Black passed over Boatshed he wished us a good morning, which salutation we returned with a wave. "Have you got any fish?" greeted Dorothy via his loudspeaker as she was fishing.

Dorothy combined business with pleasure when out in the dinghy with her rod, and on occasion, when her catch was big enough, fish was on the menu for the passing track parties.

A few trampers carried their rods and tried their luck in the brief time at their disposal. An American came down from Park Board Hut one evening near nightfall. As supplies were running low, he had promised his mates fish for breakfast when he had cooked the last of the oatmeal that morning, so looking in at the river here and there on the way down he found a few spots for casting but no fish. Dorothy took him in the dinghy up to the first rapids and to his surprise and pleasure he hooked and landed a four-pounder on his first cast. With a two-pound trout that Dorothy caught he happily made his way back in the dark to his starving companions.

Fish are there in plenty, both great and small. Mike Cramond hooked a nine-pounder, a beauty, half a mile above Boatshed one evening, just as he was ready to call it a day. It fought to such effect it broke his rod. Considering it had earned its freedom he returned it to the stream.

There is, or was, a twenty-pound trout in the deep water at the bend below Boatshed. As I was going down the river in the dinghy, this outsize specimen surfaced, but with head and tail submerged. "What can that be?" I said to myself, never thinking it could be a trout. On rare occasions a seal found its way up as far as Boatshed. "Could this possibly be portion of its bulk displayed above the water-line?"

I would still be wondering had I not been favoured with a good look at it, as it swam away in the clear water near the boat.

A few others have seen it and their estimate of its size corresponds with mine. One of these times a lucky angler may be able to check its weight on the scales.

To make it easier to reach the sandbanks on foot from Boatshed, I cleared the track and blasted some rock where a slip had carried away the track at the bluff. Then three-quarters of a mile above

Boatshed at Diamond Creek I cut a track leading to the shingle banks lower down. Whether with or without a boat, these reaches above and below Boatshed make first-class fishing spots. From that shingle area I continued on with the track, following the sweep of the river down to Boatshed. This portion, however, needs more work put into it.

With a more serviceable track from Diamond Creek to Boatshed, trampers coming down with a rod would more happily fish their way on that mile than stick to the main track.

Taking Dorothy's brother George with me I paid Quintin and the Pass another visit. At Quintin we found Mr Connelly and his men putting the machinery together. In a remarkably brief space of time each part found its counterpart and they were ready for work. As so often happens, the weather improved immediately the last track party went through. With bright sunshine to cheer them the men were all eager to get on with the job. Some members of the track staff remained to join them: Joy Hewitt, as victualler, Bill Hewitt, Dane Woods and Peter McBride to man the various machines.

The winter closed in on them and, apart from a brief letter from Bill Hewitt, we heard nothing more of them until early in July when we were told that they had all come out. We left Boatshed on 24 April, having waited to cater for a late fishing party. After spending twelve days at Hollyford Camp, allowing Murray Gunn to attend to some business towards the end of May, we settled down at home in Invercargill for the winter.

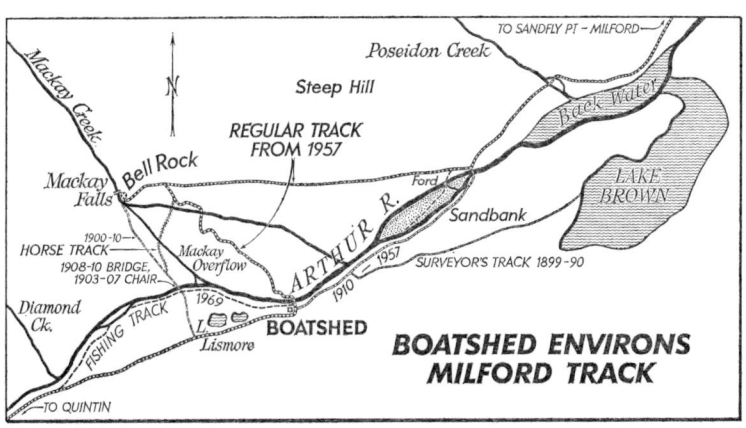

19

STILL THE FINEST WALK

IN AUGUST 1969 my son Bert took over Cascade Lodge and instead of visiting Sandfly as we usually did we put in odd times there.

On 22 September Mr Connelly, the contractor, called in at Cascade and asked me if I would care to go in with him to Quintin. I very willingly joined him. We spent the night at Milford to be ready if an early flight might be possible, and the day, when the early mists dispersed, was wonderfully fine. The plane, piloted by Rex Smith, shuttled back and forth between Milford and Quintin carrying mostly diesel. I went in on the second trip. This was my first flight up the Arthur Valley, and as a scenic flight it was wonderful. The height at which we flew revealed much that is hidden from walking the Track. The upper reaches of Joe's River and the creeks entering the Arthur River from the west, were all spread out clearly below us, beautiful and impressive. The strip was still in the making but was nearing completion. Bill Hewitt was still there but this was his last day: he went out on one of the return flights to Milford. He served the last of the hundreds of meals he so skilfully provided in his seven years as manager and chef at Quintin.

In selecting illustrations for this book, there were some slides of Zygmunt Kepka's I wanted to make use of so wrote to him for permission to use them. Not only did he say yes but generously offered to come down from Wellington to obtain more up-to-date ones for me if I could see that a visit to the Track could be arranged. Permission was readily given by the manager of Hotel Te Anau, Mr Hanreats, and Mr Withington of Hotel Milford. Dorothy, Zyg and I were on our way in to Milford when the rain started. By the time we reached the Homer Tunnel it seemed to mean business, so we turned back and spent the night at Hollyford Camp. As it was still raining the next day, we decided against going on the Track until the weather cleared. We made for home, passing through water here and there where it was running across or

174

gathered on the road. We spent Christmas 1969 with the young folk and on the following Monday set off again, caught the launch going over to Sandfly for a track party and from there made our way up to Boatshed.

The next day the weather was dull and, as he could find no profitable use for his camera, Zyg set to work and lowered one of the bunks perched high up near the ceiling in the fishing lodge. I went three-quarters of a mile up the track where, during the previous season, I had cut a track to enable fishermen to reach the wide shingle banks some three or four hundred yards below the entry of Diamond Creek. There was a fair amount of driftwood to clear off the track, brought there by recent floods.

As the following day, Wednesday, looked promising, Zyg set off at 5 am for the MacKinnon Pass. Dorothy and I waited to attend to a track party and put them across the river before making our way up to Quintin.

We were made very welcome by Mr and Mrs Turnbull and found Quintin in very good hands, all the staff contributing something towards that homely, friendly atmosphere which means so much to the wayfarer. As the weather remained persistently poor for photography, Zyg armed himself with a pick and shovel, cleared out all the run-offs and watertables on the Pass track and tackled the construction of a new stretch at Roaring Creek which had undermined and collapsed during the last flood.

I went up to give him a hand to complete it. The drizzle of the morning gradually became heavier until we were soaked and plastered with mud which appeared as a by-product from our effort to make a new ledge on the near-perpendicular bank. "What a way to spend a holiday," remarked Zyg. Nevertheless, I think he was pleased at seeing a serviceable track emerge from our labours.

One day Mr and Mrs Turnbull, Pauline, their daughter, Dorothy and I went round the Anderson Track to the Christie Falls bridge then down the River track on the way back. Without an additional day at Quintin, trampers could not make use of this most alluring track, and consequently it had not been cleared. In places it was difficult to make a way through. At the Giant's Castle one of the underground passages was completely blocked with driftwood and rubble, while another, after the removal of some of the lighter timber, allowed us to worm our way through on our tummies.

175

There was a good flow of water in the river, showing to advantage the turbulent stretches, cascades and waterfalls.

Returning to Quintin there was enough of the afternoon left to invite Dorothy and me to look over a route continuing on from the Triple Falls to reach the main Falls Track some distance up the ridge from the top of which the Sutherland Falls comes into view. We blazed a way for this section of new track and later opened it up enough to follow without much difficulty. A close-up view of the Triple Falls is quite impressive and the new track leaving that point avoids the trouble of doubling back when on the way up to see the Sutherland Falls.

Zyg worked away as opportunity offered to get his photographs, ranging over the track as far as Glade House. Dorothy and I went over to Pompolona and were agreeably surprised to meet, coming down from the Pass as we ascended, a previous track walker I had known as Ruth Gill. We had met her American husband before encountering Ruth and her sister.

At Pompolona we were made to feel at home by our hostess Marlene Roostov and by Richard Tubman. The next day Richard took Dorothy and me down the new road in the jeep from where the road leaves the old track near Pompolona to the Eight Mile where it rejoins it.

We came back on foot up the old track and from the little knoll which gives a view of the "Prairie", overlooked the flat open land where the Pompolona airstrip is to be formed. In the distance the horses were idly grazing, enjoying the work-free days on the last year before banishment.

In the evening the track certificates were awarded as usual by Phil Turnbull. Trampers were also given a questionnaire, inviting expressions of opinion on the way each would like to do the Track. The questions were mainly concerned with finding out at which place the extra day should be spent on the Track, and if an extra day should be given. Their opinions were also sought on the relative value of a night spent at Glade with a full day to reach Pompolona, or, as at present, arriving at Glade about midday, leaving a half-day in which to walk it. A one or two nights' stay at Milford was another choice. One weakness in the questionnaire was the inability of many to assess the advantage an extra day would give when they were ignorant of the manner in which the day would be spent.

When the extra day was spent at Quintin in previous years, the verdict of the trampers was unqualified approval. With full daily parties, it is obvious that an additional day on the Track will mean doubling up accommodation at the favoured lodge. It has been suggested that Boatshed could be extended to give overnight accommodation. After a day's sightseeing round Quintin, there would still be time to reach Boatshed in the daylight after an early dinner. A party leaving Boatshed early in the day could be taken down the Sound for a cruise before landing at Milford. One difficulty there would be the need to provide a regular supply service from Milford, as this had been stopped when the airstrip came into use at Quintin.

Whatever pattern evolves from the experimentation of recent times, it should be possible to combine sound, economic track management with ideal service. The main needs are not obscure or beyond reach. First, to make sure of the retention of a conscientious friendly staff. Second, not too hurried a passage through the Track and third, a well-surfaced track that will allow the eyes to see something of the scenery while the feet are in motion. A wise and sympathetic overall management with some continuity of policy would achieve this ideal. And dare we venture to prophesy that sane finance will yet emerge to combat rising track costs which plague the management and penalise track patrons.

We New Zealanders may justly take pride in our Milford Track, but what is of greater importance to our overseas visitors is the kind of treatment that goes with it. If the quality of our hospitality never falls below that of the scenery then we shall always retain "The Finest Walk in the World".

In our short lives we see mountain scenery as changeless, but here on the Track are plain signs of a constant movement in the longer and shorter cycle of destruction and regeneration. Here, too, we can read the longer chapter, beginning with marks left behind from the moving glacier, followed by the mighty forces of earthquake, avalanche and flood.

I have heard many a tramper say, "Now I have seen the Track I am satisfied. I wouldn't want to go over it again!" These people, mostly fully appreciative of what they have seen, yet view it as a beautifully illustrated book but printed in an unknown foreign tongue. To see the Track is one thing, to know it another. If I were to catechise a tramper I would say: "You have seen the

Clinton River quietly, peacefully, soothingly flowing round each graceful bend, green forest above matched by the greenness of its tinted waters and mottled bed, but have you seen it on a sunny day, the mists rising from its waters, coloured in all the tints and shades from lighter to deeper blue, emerald green and violet? Have you seen the mountainsides in the Clinton canyon streaming with a thousand waterfalls? Have you been on the MacKinnon Pass on a bright, calm day, the distant mountain tops clear-cut against the deep blue sky and reflected in a score of tarns? Have you seen the after-glow of the setting sun cast a mantle of rose-red over the Lady of the Snows?

"You may have seen all this and more, yet you have seen only the superficial features. They have told you nothing of the significance of what is happening today, or what the future holds in store. There is always something new to learn and this, instead of narrowing the field left to explore, actually widens it."

Very many realise this and long for more time to find and absorb the great store of beauty and interest found here. They find, however, that they are expected to regard the Track like life, a bridge to pass over, not to build upon. The guide's admonition to keep moving, with long practice has enabled him to say it in a hundred ways, without losing one fraction of its intended meaning.

Tourists cannot buy our mountains, rivers and lakes but they do spend their money to our advantage and also, we hope, to theirs. We find that while it may be the scenery which attracts them once they are here, it is our people that arouse their greater interest. If we regard our visitors in terms of dollar-earners we may find both our dollars and our friends desert us. Their appraisal of our scenery may frequently be casual, but not so the summing up of their hosts. We cannot sell our scenery without putting a price on our heads.

The people going through the Track are good ambassadors for their different countries. It is up to us to welcome them with our most generous hospitality, and I am glad to say that with few exceptions members of the track staff have made worthy hosts. Track walkers I have known are scattered throughout the world and when their place of abode appears in the headline news I am more interested and concerned in it because of their possible involvement. It could well be that the greatest dividends the Track has earned for us have come from good fellowship engendered when people from many nations meet as strangers, and part as friends.

INDEX

Illustrations in squared brackets

179

Index

O'Brien, R., [113], 160
Orbell, Dr, 64

Pass Huts, [65], 71, 121, 133, 167
Philip Laing, 27
piano, [81], 112-18, 127
Pillans, W. S., 33-4, 38
Pompolona, 63, 71, 143; road, 164-8
Porter, Dr, 52
Poseidon Creek, 123; Hut, 41
Price, E., 60
Prison Camp, 54
prisoners, 53; grave of prisoner, 161

Quill, Lake, 48
Quill, W., 41
Quintin, [32], 20-1, 127-8

Racecourse Flat, 115, 157
Rawson, J., 115, 137
Reid, Miss, 69
Ripple, 50, 64
Roaring Creek, 40, 115
Robertson, G., 12
Robinson, I., 31
Ross, D., 61, 63; Ross, J., 13, 63, 64

Safe Cove, 36
Sandfly Point, [79], 17-18, 70-1, 142, 159
Seddon, Hon. R. J., 54, 57
Six Mile Inn, 160, 164
Slip Camp, 41, 62
Smith, H. G., 60
Snodgrass, W., 50, 56

Staircase Creek, 34
Star, Cess, 149, 155
Stella, 29
Stephen, Lake, [64]
Stevens, S., 56, 61
Stirling Falls, 28
Stokes, J. L., 26
Sutherland, D., [48], 28-9, 31-6, 39, 69
Sutherland Falls, 11, 21, 30-4, 40, 48, 91

Takahe, 64
Tarawera, 43
Tawera, [48], 64-5, 70, 74
Te Anau, 49
Te Anau Downs, 35, 36
telephones, 67
Te Uira, 46, 50, 64
Three Mile Hut, 86
Tourist Hotel Corporation, 136
track certificates, 136
tractor, 72, 140, 145
Triple Falls, 176
Tubman, R., 165
Turnbull, Mr and Mrs, 175
Tutaneki, 70

Upper Landing, 40

Wanganella, 74
Wellington, HMS, 74
Willet, R., 160
Williams, Capt. P., 26
Williams, E., 114
Wilson, I., 144
Wyinks, 37, 38

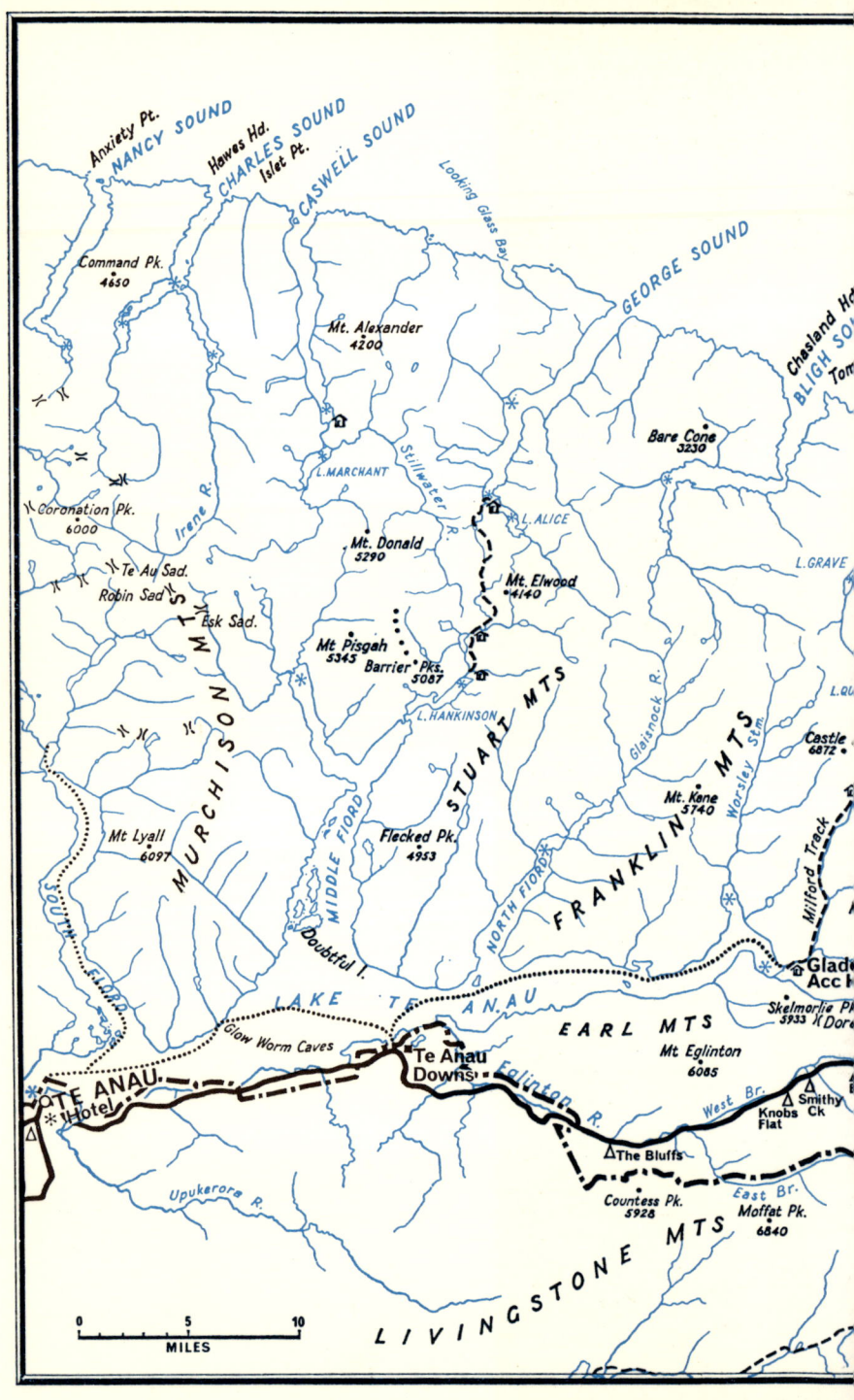

B. & L. FOLEY
P.O. BOX 574
ALICE SPRINGS, N.T., 5750
PHONE 22 051

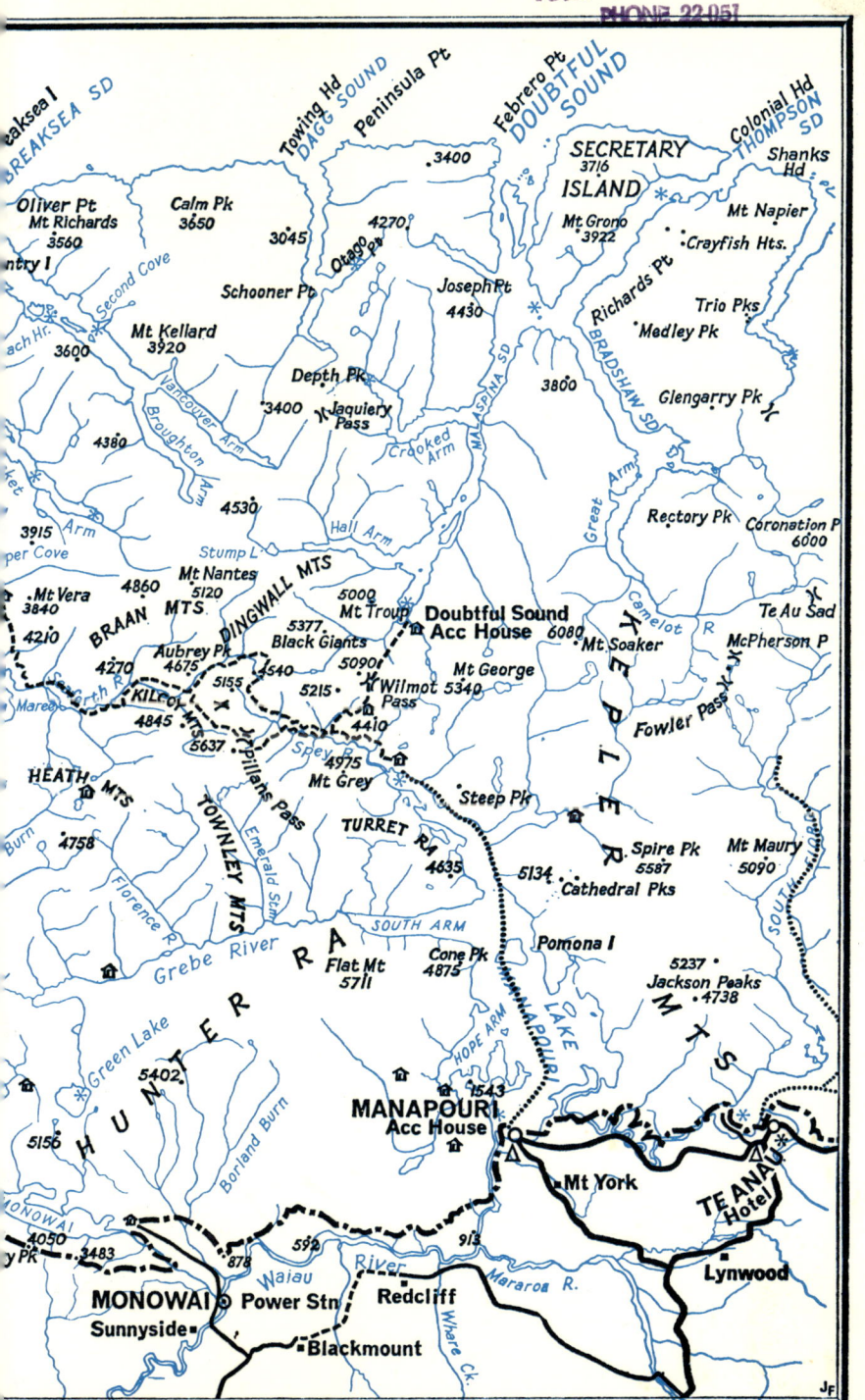